NOTE

1. All recipes serve four unless otherwise stated.

2. All spoon measurements are level.

3. All eggs are sizes 3 or 4 unless otherwise stated.

4. Preparation times given are an average calculated during recipe testing.

5. Metric and imperial measurements have been calculated separately. Use one set of measurements only as they are not exact equivalents.

6. Cooking times may vary slightly depending on the individual oven. Dishes should be placed in the centre of the oven unless otherwise specified.

7. Always preheat the oven or grill to the specified temperature.

8. Spoon measures can be bought in both imperial and metric sizes to give accurate measurement of small quantities.

Chinese Cooking

Chinese Cooking
Deh-ta Hsiung

TREASURE PRESS

Contents

First published in 1980 by
Sundial Publications Ltd

This edition published in 1984 by
Treasure Press
59 Grosvenor Street
London W1

© 1980 Hennerwood Publications Ltd

Reprinted 1986

ISBN 0 907812 77 5

Printed in Hong Kong

前言

INTRODUCTION

**'To be a good cook, one must first be a
good matchmaker who understands
harmony and the marriage of different
flavours.'**

– Chinese proverb

This old saying more or less sums up the
essence of Chinese cooking: for the secret
of this ancient art lies not so much in
mastering the few basic techniques – but
in what to cook. The most important
aspect of Chinese cooking is the blending
of ingredients to achieve a harmonized
contrast in colour, flavour and texture.
Here you will find over ninety recipes
using ingredients easily obtained from
supermarkets or specialist food stores.
They have been chosen for their tastiness
and ease in preparation, and in some cases
adapted for the Western kitchen.
The recipes have been selected from the
four main regions of cuisine in China;
each area makes the best use of its natural
products and has developed its own
regional variations of cuisine: Peking in
the north, where many of the lamb dishes
come from, for instance, Lamb and
Spring Onions (page 48), and garlic and
leeks are a favourite ingredient; Shanghai
in the east, where the use of sugar is
prevalent in the cooking; Sichuan in the
west, where many of the piquant and hot,
spicy dishes using chillies originate from;
and Canton in the south, which offers the
widest variety of food, particularly pork,
for instance, Roast Crispy Pork (page 42),
and seafood, for instance, Squid and
Green Peppers (page 24).

用料處理

Preparing the food
When preparing food for a Chinese recipe
it is important that the different
ingredients to be served together in one
dish should be cut into uniformly small
pieces. There are two reasons for this.
Firstly, to achieve harmony in appearance
as well as in texture, and secondly, the
prepared food will require only a matter of
minutes or even seconds to cook through,
thus the natural flavours are preserved.
No special equipment is needed to prepare
the food, but a good sharp knife is
essential. When the recipe calls for slices,
this means that the ingredient should be
cut to the size of a large postage stamp and
as thin as cardboard. When it calls for
shreds or thin strips, the ingredient
should be cut into matchstick-sized
pieces. Dicing means the ingredient is
first cut into strips the size of a potato
chip, then cubed.
Meat should be sliced across the grain,
and it is easier to cut thin slices off the
meat if it is half frozen, but it should be
thawed thoroughly before cooking to
ensure tenderness and natural flavour.
Cutting vegetables diagonally increases
the surface which comes into contact with
the hot oil while being cooked. This
ensures fast cooking and preserves the
texture and the flavour.
After the meat is cut, it is often mixed
with cornflour to form a light outer
coating which prevents the juice from
escaping when it is cooked and at the same
time helps to keep the meat tender.

Planning and serving a meal

At a Chinese meal, all the dishes are served at once, and placed in the centre of the table. Each person has a medium-sized plate, a bowl for rice and soup, a porcelain spoon and a pair of chopsticks with which they help themselves from the central dishes. One of the advantages of Chinese food is the way it 'stretches', and an extra pair of chopsticks and another bowl of rice will accommodate an unexpected guest. For this reason, it is rather difficult to give precise 'helpings' for each recipe. As a rule of thumb, allow one dish for each person. If you are cooking for only two or three people, serve one meat dish, one vegetable and rice, plus a soup if desired. For an informal meal for four to six people, serve four dishes plus soup and rice; for a formal dinner there should be six to eight dishes.

When cooking for more people always increase the number of dishes rather than the quantity of ingredients, as this offers more variety on the table.

When planning a meal, choose two, at the most three stir-fry dishes (which must be served immediately) together with steamed, stewed, roasted, braised or cold dishes which can all be prepared in advance to some extent. In this way you will have time to enjoy the meal, and not be constantly in the kitchen.

Most of the recipes in this book can also be served in the Western manner, either on their own or in conjunction with non-Chinese food. For instance, some of the poultry and meat dishes can be served together with rice or pasta and vegetables. Equally, almost any of the vegetable dishes in this book could go with your Sunday joint or a non-Chinese supper.

Methods of cooking and equipment

One of the most frequent methods of cooking in China is *stir-frying*. This is a very quick method of cooking, similar to the Western method of shallow-frying. The correct utensil for this technique is a sloping-sided heavy metal pan called a *wok*, but any large frying pan or saucepan will do. However, a wok would be a very useful utensil to have in the kitchen; it is ideal as a base for a Chinese bamboo steamer and can also serve as a deep-fryer. Stir-frying is easy to do once you know how. It is important to remember that the oil must be extremely hot and the ingredients uniformly small, so that the cooking can be done very quickly – success lies in the right heat and timing.

To stir-fry, heat a wok or frying pan, pour in a few tablespoons of oil and heat it until it is very hot. Add the ingredients and stir and toss them constantly for a very short time using a large long-handled wooden or metal spoon. All this stirring makes sure that every part is in contact with the hot oil so the natural juices are sealed in and the food is crisp and not overcooked. Dishes cooked this way are best served immediately.

Steaming is another favourite cooking method in China. The Chinese use bamboo steamers which allow a certain amount of evaporation because they are not airtight, and so prevent condensation forming inside the lid.

There are two methods of steaming: firstly, a plate or bowl containing the ingredients is placed on the perforated rack of the steamer. The steamer is then put inside a wok or on top of a large pot containing boiling water so that the steam passing through the steamer cooks the items of food.

The second method is to immerse the pot or bowl of ingredients part-way into the boiling water, rather like a double saucepan, and the cooking action is performed both by the boiling water and the rising steam.

Deep-frying is another common method of Chinese food preparation. For this a wok, deep-fryer or a saucepan with a wire basket which fits inside it is most convenient.

Chinese cooking also uses methods such as stewing, braising, shallow-frying, boiling or roasting, which are very little different from the way in which they are used in European cooking.

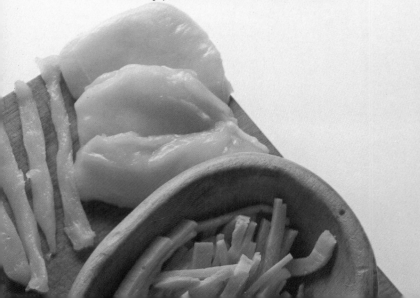

What to drink

As wine enhances the enjoyment of any food, there is no reason why you should not drink it with your meal, and you will find some suggested wines to serve with the sample menus on pages 10 to 11. A light beer or lager is equally suitable. In China people drink tea almost all day long, but seldom with their meals. So serve China tea without sugar or milk instead of coffee at the end of a meal, it is most refreshing and invigorating.

Using chopsticks

Using chopsticks is very simple:

1. Place the first chopstick in the hollow between thumb and index finger and rest its lower end below the first joint of the third finger. This chopstick remains stationary.

2. Hold the other chopstick between the tips of the index and middle fingers, steady its upper half against the base of the index finger, and use the tip of the thumb to keep it in place.

3. To pick up food, move the upper chopstick with the index and the middle fingers.

If the chopsticks seem difficult to manipulate at first, practise with them away from the dinner table. Otherwise eat Chinese food with a fork or spoon.

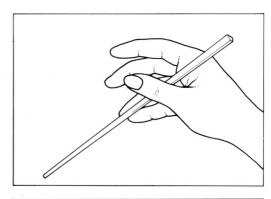

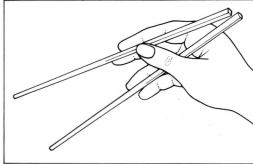

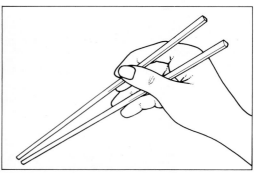

Special ingredients

特種原料

The following is a guide to the more frequently used Chinese ingredients:

Bamboo shoots: available in cans only in this country. Once the can is opened the shoots may be kept immersed in water in a covered jar for up to a week in the refrigerator. Courgettes or asparagus can be substituted for texture, but not flavour.

Bean-curd: will keep for a few days if submerged in water in a container and placed in the coldest part of a refrigerator. There is no substitute.

Bean-sprouts: fresh bean-sprouts can be kept in the refrigerator for two to three days. Canned bean-sprouts do not have the crunchy texture which is the main characteristic of this popular vegetable.

Chinese dried mushrooms: widely used in many dishes as a complementary vegetable for their flavour and aroma. Soak them in a bowl of warm water for 20 to 30 minutes, squeeze dry and discard the hard stalks before use. Continental dried mushrooms, though of slightly different flavour and fragrance can be a substitute, use fresh field mushrooms for texture.

Sichuan preserved vegetable: is the root of a very special variety of the mustard green pickled in salt and chilli. Sold in cans, once opened it can be stored in a tightly sealed jar in the refrigerator for months. There is no substitute.

Water chestnuts: available both fresh or in cans. Canned water chestnuts are peeled and will keep for several weeks in a refrigerator in a covered jar. There is no substitute.

Wooden ears: also known as black fungus. They should be soaked in a bowl of warm water for 20 minutes then rinsed in fresh water before use. They have a crunchy texture and a mild but subtle flavour. There is no substitute.

Special seasonings

特種調味料

Certain spices and seasonings are indispensable in the Chinese kitchen. They are used to enrich the flavour of the food and should not overpower it. The more important seasonings are:

Bean sauce: a thickish sauce made from black or yellow soya beans, flour and salt. It is sold in tins and once opened must be transferred into a screw-top jar; it will then keep in a refrigerator for at least 3 months. Bovril can be substituted in recipes calling for only a tablespoon or less of bean sauce, but not in those using more.

Chilli purée: made of chilli, soya bean, salt, sugar and flour, it is sold in jars and will keep almost indefinitely. Chilli sauce or Tabasco sauce can be substituted, but remember to use half the quantity as they are twice as strong.

Cooking oil: a Chinese cook's favourite oil for cooking is peanut oil, followed by soya bean, rape seed or other vegetable oils. Lard and chicken fat are sometimes used but not butter or dripping.

Five-spice powder: a mixture of star anise, fennel seed, cloves, cinnamon and pepper, it is very strongly piquant, so use it sparingly. You can make your own by grinding together about 4 star anise (or the equivalent in pieces), 2×5 ml spoons (2 teaspoons) fennel seed, 12 cloves, 4 cinnamon sticks (each no longer than 2.5 cm/1 inch), 2×5 ml spoons (2 teaspoons) Sichuan or white peppercorns and 1×5 ml spoon (1 teaspoon) ground ginger (optional).

Ginger root: sold by weight, should be peeled and sliced or finely chopped before use. It will keep for several weeks in a dry, cool place. Dried ginger root is much stronger so use less in quantity, but ground ginger has a quite different flavour and therefore is no substitute.

Hoi sin sauce: is also known as barbecue sauce. It is available ready-made or you can make your own from 3×15 ml spoons (3 tablespoons) yellow bean sauce, 2×15 ml spoons (2 tablespoons) sugar, 1×15 ml spoon (1 tablespoon) vinegar, a crushed garlic clove, 1×5 ml spoon (1 teaspoon) chilli sauce and 1×15 ml spoon (1 tablespoon) sesame seed oil.

Oyster sauce: a thick sauce made from oysters and soy sauce. Sold in bottles, it will keep in the refrigerator for several months.

Sesame seed oil: sold in bottles and widely used in China as a garnish rather than for cooking. The refined yellow sesame oil sold in Middle Eastern stores is not so aromatic, has less flavour, and is not a very satisfactory substitute.

Sherry: is widely used as a good substitute for rice wine, which is unobtainable in this country. Use a pale, dry sherry rather than a sweet one.

Soy sauce: sold in bottles or cans, this most popular Chinese sauce ranges from light to dark brown with varying strength.

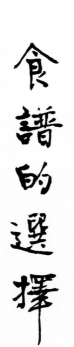

Choosing a meal
Many people are bewildered by the menu in a Chinese restaurant when faced with a vast range of choices. What at first appears to be a rather puzzling order of serving different dishes or courses is, in fact, a carefully worked out programme based on the Chinese conception of harmony: a balanced contrast of colour, flavour and texture.

A well-balanced Chinese dinner should include all three 'meats': fish, poultry and pork or beef. These three main ingredients are supplemented by others to form anything from six up to twelve carefully selected dishes. Therefore the wine or wines you choose to serve with these dishes should also complement each other as well as the food.

Suggested menus for a family of 4 to 6:

Menu A
Prawns fu-yung
Stewed lamb
Chinese cabbage in a creamy sauce
Chicken and mushroom soup (optional)
Plain rice

Menu B
Fried fish slices
Chicken and bean-sprouts
Green peppers stuffed with pork
Spinach and bean-curd
Egg-flower soup or Beef and tomato soup
Plain rice

Wine to serve: choose either a red or white wine for both menus – a light and fruity Beaujolais would be ideal, or a medium-bodied white such as a Riesling.

四盤一湯兩大菜宴席

Suggested menus for an informal dinner to serve 6 to 8 people:

Menu A
Prawns and green peas
Chicken and bean-sprouts
Fried pork liver
Broccoli pieces in oyster sauce
Pork, ham and bamboo shoot soup
Braised lamb chops
Sweet and sour fish
Plain rice

Menu B
Boiled chicken
Fried prawn balls
Aubergines in fragrant sauce
Beef and onions
Sweetcorn and crab soup
Pork in fragrant sauce
Braised carp
Plain rice

Wine to serve: at least two bottles of wine are called for – a white and a red. The white can either be a Hock or Alsace, the red should be a full-bodied Burgundy or Côtes-du-Rhône.

四冷盤四熱葷四大菜一湯一甜點心筵席

Suggested menus for a formal dinner to serve 10 to 12 people:

4 cold dishes to be served simultaneously:
Soy chicken
Braised prawns in shells
Roast crispy pork
Celery salad

4 hot dishes to be served one at a time:
Fried prawns in batter
Diced chicken with peppers
Pork with mushrooms and bamboo shoots
Sliced beef in oyster sauce

Soup:
Bean-curd and prawn soup
or Hot and sour soup

4 main dishes to be served one at a time:
Braised duck
Braised leg of pork
Chinese cabbage and mushrooms
Steamed whole fish

Dessert:
Almond junket or Toffee apples

Rice is optional for a banquet of this dimension, usually everybody is too full to touch it.

Wine to serve: you will need 4 to 6 bottles of wine. To start with, serve a lightish white such as a Muscadet, Graves or Mâcon to be followed by a fuller and fruitier Alsace or white Burgundy. The reds offer a very wide choice, all depend on the occasion and your budget. You can either stick to a good Beaujolais or lash out on a Burgundy such as Chambolle-Musigny, Nuits-St-Georges or a Beaune. For claret lovers try a full-bodied St. Emilion or a Pomerol rather than a Médoc.

Spinach and bean-curd; Egg-flower soup; Chicken and bean-sprouts; Plain rice

SOUPS

At an everyday meal, the Chinese serve a simply made clear soup together with other dishes. On a formal occasion, the soup will appear at the end of the meal or indeed during the middle of it – to serve as a neutralizer between courses, in order to clean one's palate.

There is no need for you to break the Western tradition of serving soup at the beginning of your meal. As a compromise, you can always add some boiling water or clear stock to whatever is left from the main dish at the end of a meal and serve it up as an instant soup, as most housewives in China would do.

Stock (clear soup)

Metric	Imperial
2.75 litres water	*5 pints water*
450 g chicken pieces	*1 lb chicken pieces*
450 g pork spare ribs	*1 lb pork spare ribs*

Traditionally, the best stock is made by gently simmering a whole chicken, a whole duck and a leg of ham or pork. After four hours or so when the liquid is reduced by at least one third, the stock is strained and all the ingredients are discarded. This, in the days of high food prices, seems to be rather extravagant. The recipe has, therefore, been modified somewhat. A chicken stock cube made up with water in the usual way may be used instead, but the flavour will not be as good, and the amount of salt used in the recipe should be reduced.

Bring the water to the boil in a large pot, place the chicken pieces and pork spare ribs in it, bring back to the boil and remove any scum that rises to the surface. Reduce the heat, then partially cover the pan and simmer gently for at least 2 hours or until the liquid is reduced by about one third. Leave to cool before straining, and when the stock is cold, remove the caked fat from the surface.
This stock will keep in the refrigerator for about a week, but if the weather is warm, boil it up every two or three days.

Sweetcorn and crab soup

Metric	Imperial
1×5 ml spoon finely chopped ginger root	*1 teaspoon finely chopped ginger root*
100 g crab meat	*4 oz crab meat*
2×5 ml spoons sherry	*2 teaspoons sherry*
1 egg white	*1 egg white*
3×5 ml spoons cornflour	*3 teaspoons cornflour*
2×15 ml spoons cold water	*2 tablespoons cold water*
600 ml Stock	*1 pint Stock*
1×5 ml spoon salt	*1 teaspoon salt*
100 g sweetcorn	*4 oz sweetcorn*
1 spring onion, finely chopped, to garnish	*1 spring onion, finely chopped, to garnish*

Preparation time: about 15 minutes

Mix the ginger root with the crab meat and sherry. Beat the egg white and mix the cornflour with the water to a smooth paste.
Bring the stock to a rolling boil, then add the salt, sweetcorn and crab meat. When it starts to boil again, add the cornflour and water mixture, stirring constantly. Add the egg white, stirring, and garnish with finely chopped spring onion. Serve hot.

Stock; Sweetcorn and crab soup

Chicken and mushroom soup

Metric	Imperial
100 g chicken breast meat	4 oz chicken breast meat
salt	salt
2×5 ml spoons cornflour	2 teaspoons cornflour
1 egg white	1 egg white
50 g mushrooms	2 oz mushrooms
50 g bamboo shoots	2 oz bamboo shoots
600 ml Stock (page 13)	1 pint Stock (page 13)
1×15 ml spoon soy sauce	1 tablespoon soy sauce

Preparation time: 20 minutes

Thinly slice the chicken breast meat, mix with a pinch of salt, the cornflour and egg white. Cut the mushrooms and bamboo shoots into thin slices.
Bring the stock to a rolling boil, put in the chicken, mushrooms and bamboo shoots, then add the soy sauce. When the soup starts to boil again and all the ingredients float to the surface, it is ready to serve.

Chicken and mushroom soup; Egg-flower soup;
Bean-curd and prawn soup

Egg-flower soup

Metric	Imperial
a few wooden ears	a few wooden ears
100 g pork fillet	4 oz pork fillet
1×15 ml spoon soy sauce	1 tablespoon soy sauce
1×5 ml spoon cornflour	1 teaspoon cornflour
1 egg	1 egg
1×5 ml spoon salt	1 teaspoon salt
600 ml Stock (page 13)	1 pint Stock (page 13)

Preparation time: 20 to 25 minutes

Soak the wooden ears in water for 15 to 20 minutes, then rinse them. Cut the pork into thin slices then mix with the soy sauce and cornflour. Beat the egg with a pinch of the salt until frothy.
Bring the stock to the boil, then put in the wooden ears followed by the pork. When it starts to boil again, pour in the beaten egg, stirring constantly. Bring to the boil again, add the remaining salt and serve.

Variation:
To create the traditional effect of the egg separating into strands, have the soup at a rapid boil before pouring in the beaten egg (see picture on page 10).

Bean-curd and prawn soup

Metric	Imperial
50 g peeled prawns	2 oz peeled prawns
1 egg white	1 egg white
50 g cooked ham	2 oz cooked ham
1 cake of bean-curd	1 cake of bean-curd
600 ml Stock (page 13)	1 pint Stock (page 13)
50 g green peas	2 oz green peas
1×15 ml spoon soy sauce	1 tablespoon soy sauce
1×15 ml spoon cornflour	1 tablespoon cornflour
salt	salt
freshly ground black pepper	freshly ground black pepper

Preparation time: about 15 minutes

Mix the peeled prawns with the egg white. Cut the ham and bean-curd into small cubes roughly the same size as the green peas.
Bring the stock to the boil, put in the ham, bean-curd and green peas; when it starts to bubble again, add the soy sauce and prawns, then let it boil for 15 to 20 seconds.
Mix the cornflour with a little cold water and pour it into the soup, stirring constantly. Allow to thicken, then add salt and pepper before serving.

Hot and sour soup

Metric
3 Chinese dried mushrooms
100 g pork fillet
1 cake of bean-curd
50 g Sichuan preserved
  vegetable
600 ml Stock (page 13) or
  water
1×15 ml spoon sherry
1×15 ml spoon soy sauce
freshly ground black pepper
1×15 ml spoon wine vinegar
1×5 ml spoon salt

Imperial
3 Chinese dried mushrooms
4 oz pork fillet
1 cake of bean-curd
2 oz Sichuan preserved
  vegetable
1 pint Stock (page 13) or
  water
1 tablespoon sherry
1 tablespoon soy sauce
freshly ground black pepper
1 tablespoon wine vinegar
1 teaspoon salt

Preparation time: about 20 minutes

Soak the mushrooms in warm water for 20 minutes, then squeeze dry. Discard the hard stalks, then cut the mushrooms into thin shreds. Thinly shred the pork, bean-curd and Sichuan preserved vegetable.
Bring the stock or water to the boil, drop in the pork, mushrooms, bean-curd and Sichuan preserved vegetable. Simmer for 2 minutes, then add the sherry, soy sauce, pepper and vinegar and salt.

Variation:
If you prefer a thicker soup simply mix 2×5 ml spoons (2 teaspoons) cornflour to a smooth paste with 1×15 ml spoon (1 tablespoon) water and stir into the soup at the end. Cook for 1 or 2 minutes.

Beef and tomato soup

Metric
100 g beef steak
1½×5 ml spoons salt
1×5 ml spoon cornflour
225 g tomatoes
600 ml Stock (page 13)

Imperial
4 oz beef steak
1½ teaspoons salt
1 teaspoon cornflour
8 oz tomatoes
1 pint Stock (page 13)

Preparation time: about 20 minutes

Thinly slice the beef steak and mix the strips with a pinch of the salt and all the cornflour. Slice the tomatoes, which can either be skinned or have their skins left on, as you wish.
Bring the stock to a rolling boil, put in the beef steak and tomato slices, add the remaining salt and let it bubble for 1 minute before serving.

Pork, ham and bamboo shoot soup

Metric
50 g pork fillet
2×5 ml spoons soy sauce
50 g cooked ham
50 g bamboo shoots
600 ml Stock (page 13)
1×5 ml spoon salt
1×5 ml spoon sherry

Imperial
2 oz pork fillet
2 teaspoons soy sauce
2 oz cooked ham
2 oz bamboo shoots
1 pint Stock (page 13)
1 teaspoon salt
1 teaspoon sherry

Preparation time: about 20 minutes

Thinly slice the pork and mix it with the soy sauce. Shred the ham and bamboo shoots.
Bring the stock to the boil, put in the pork, ham and bamboo shoots. When the soup starts to boil again, add the salt and sherry and serve hot.

Variation:
If you prefer a thicker soup simply mix 2×5 ml spoons (2 teaspoons) cornflour to a smooth paste with 1×15 ml spoon (1 tablespoon) water and stir into the soup at the end. Cook for 1 or 2 minutes to thicken.

Left: Hot and sour soup
Right: Beef and tomato soup; Pork, ham and bamboo shoot soup

Kidney soup

Metric	Imperial
1 pork kidney or 2 lamb's kidneys	1 pork kidney or 2 lamb's kidneys
1×15 ml spoon sherry	1 tablespoon sherry
2×5 ml spoons cornflour	2 teaspoons cornflour
3-4 Chinese dried mushrooms	3-4 Chinese dried mushrooms
1 bamboo shoot	1 bamboo shoot
600 ml Stock (page 13)	1 pint Stock (page 13)
1×15 ml spoon soy sauce	1 tablespoon soy sauce
1×5 ml spoon salt	1 teaspoon salt
1 spring onion, finely chopped, to garnish	1 spring onion, finely chopped, to garnish

Preparation time: 15 to 20 minutes

Slice the kidneys in half, core and cut them into thin slices. Marinate the slices in the sherry mixed with the cornflour, for 10 minutes.
Soak the dried mushrooms in warm water for 15 minutes, squeeze dry and discard the hard stalks, then cut them into thin slices.
Cut the bamboo shoot into thin slices.
Pour the stock into a saucepan and bring to the boil. Add the kidneys, mushrooms and bamboo shoot. Stir in the soy sauce and salt, boil over a high heat for about 1½ minutes. Garnish with finely chopped spring onions and serve hot.

Spare ribs and bean-sprout soup

Metric	Imperial
100 g pork spare ribs	4 oz pork spare ribs
2 slices ginger root, peeled	2 slices ginger root, peeled
900 ml water	1½ pints water
225 g fresh bean-sprouts	8 oz fresh bean-sprouts
1 tomato, sliced	1 tomato, sliced
2×5 ml spoons salt	2 teaspoons salt
1 spring onion, finely chopped, to garnish	1 spring onion, finely chopped, to garnish

Preparation time: 10 minutes

Ask your butcher to chop each pork spare rib into 2 to 3 pieces.
Place the spare rib pieces with the ginger root in a large saucepan, add the water and bring to the boil. Reduce the heat, cover and simmer gently for about 1 hour or until the liquid is reduced by a third.
Add the bean-sprouts and the tomato.
Increase the heat to high and add the salt. Cook for about 1 minute, garnish with finely chopped spring onion and serve.

Shredded pork and spinach soup

Metric	Imperial
100 g pork fillet	4 oz pork fillet
1×5 ml spoon soy sauce	1 teaspoon soy sauce
1×5 ml spoon sugar	1 teaspoon sugar
2×5 ml spoons cornflour	2 teaspoons cornflour
175 g spinach leaves	6 oz spinach leaves
600 ml Stock (page 13)	1 pint Stock (page 13)
1×5 ml spoon salt	1 teaspoon salt

Preparation time: 10 to 15 minutes

Cut the pork into shreds the size of matchsticks. Marinate the shreds in soy sauce mixed with the sugar and cornflour, for about 10 minutes.
Wash the spinach leaves and shred them.
Pour the stock into a saucepan and bring to the boil. Add the pork, spinach and salt. Boil rapidly over a high heat for about 1 minute. Serve hot.

Shredded pork and spinach soup;
Kidney soup; Spare ribs and bean-sprout soup

FISH

The Chinese eat far more fish than meat in their daily diet, largely because of its abundance. For China not only has a long coastline but also a great number of rivers and tributaries as well as lakes and streams, not to mention the numerous ponds in the countryside which are used extensively for fish farming.

The best fish, say Chinese cooks, have bright red gills, clear eyes and flesh firm to the touch. Ideally fish should be bought still alive, but freshly frozen fish is the next best thing. Another important point to remember is not to over-cook a fish, as much of its delicate flavour will be lost if cooked too long.

Steamed whole fish

Metric	Imperial
2 Chinese dried mushrooms	2 Chinese dried mushrooms
1×450 g fish (sea bass or perch)	1×1 lb fish (sea bass or perch)
2 slices ginger root, peeled	2 slices ginger root, peeled
2 spring onions	2 spring onions
50 g cooked ham	2 oz cooked ham
50 g bamboo shoots	2 oz bamboo shoots
3×15 ml spoons sherry	3 tablespoons sherry
2×15 ml spoons soy sauce	2 tablespoons soy sauce
1×5 ml spoon sugar	1 teaspoon sugar
1×5 ml spoon salt	1 teaspoon salt

Preparation time: about 25 minutes

The Chinese like to cook their fish whole with head and tail intact. You will need a bamboo steamer not less than 33 cm (13 inches) in diameter in order to take a plate 30 cm (12 inches) long. Otherwise, halve the fish and use a round dish which will fit into a metal steamer used in the Western kitchen.

Soak the mushrooms in warm water for 20 minutes, squeeze them dry and discard the stalks.
Scale and clean the fish if it has not already been done. Slash both sides diagonally as deep as the bone at intervals of about 1 cm (½ inch). This prevents the skin from bursting in cooking, allows the heat to penetrate more quickly and helps to diffuse the flavour of the seasonings and sauce. Dry the fish well, then place it on a plate.
Thinly shred the ginger root, spring onions, ham, mushrooms and bamboo shoots, then put them on top of the fish. Mix the sherry, soy sauce, sugar and salt in a jug and pour it all over the fish. Steam vigorously for 15 minutes and serve.

Braised fish

Metric	Imperial
1×500 g fish (sea bass, grey mullet, carp or perch)	1×1¼ lb fish (sea bass, grey mullet, carp or perch)
2 slices ginger root, peeled	2 slices ginger root, peeled
1 spring onion	1 spring onion
3×15 ml spoons oil	3 tablespoons oil

Sauce:	Sauce:
3×15 ml spoons sherry	3 tablespoons sherry
3×15 ml spoons soy sauce	3 tablespoons soy sauce
1×5 ml spoon sugar	1 teaspoon sugar
1×2.5 ml spoon salt	½ teaspoon salt
2×15 ml spoons Stock (page 13) or water	2 tablespoons Stock (page 13) or water
1×2.5 ml spoon five-spice powder (optional)	½ teaspoon five-spice powder (optional)

Preparation time: about 15 minutes

Scale and clean the fish if it has not already been done. Cut it into about 3 pieces.
Thinly shred the ginger root and cut the spring onion into 2.5 cm (1 inch) lengths.
In a large heavy frying pan or wok, heat the oil until hot, then fry the fish for 5 minutes, turning the pieces once. Push the fish to one side and fry the shredded ginger root and spring onion. Mix together the sauce ingredients and add to the pan.
Return the fish to the middle of the pan. Simmer for 10 minutes, turning the fish pieces over once, very carefully, half way during simmering. This dish can be served either hot or cold.

Steamed whole fish; Braised fish

Braised carp

Metric
1 × 1 kg carp
1 × 5 ml spoon salt
2 garlic cloves
2 slices ginger root, peeled
4 spring onions
250 ml oil
2 × 15 ml spoons soy sauce
1 × 15 ml spoon sherry
1½ × 5 ml spoons sugar
300 ml Stock (page 13) or
   water
1 × 5 ml spoon cornflour
1 × 5 ml spoon sesame seed
   oil (optional)

Imperial
1 × 2 lb carp
1 teaspoon salt
2 garlic cloves
2 slices ginger root, peeled
4 spring onions
8 fl oz oil
2 tablespoons soy sauce
1 tablespoon sherry
1½ teaspoons sugar
½ pint Stock (page 13) or
   water
1 teaspoon cornflour
1 teaspoon sesame seed oil
   (optional)

Preparation time: about 20 minutes

If the carp is under 1 kg (2 lb) in weight, it is best cooked whole, otherwise it should be cut into two or three pieces.

Scale and clean the carp if it has not already been done. Slash both sides of the fish diagonally, as far as the bone, at intervals of about 1 cm (½ inch). Dry it thoroughly and rub on the salt both on the inside and outside of the fish.
Crush the garlic, thinly slice the ginger root and cut the spring onions into 2½ cm (1 inch) lengths.
In a frying pan or wok heat the oil until hot, then fry the carp for 2 minutes on each side. Remove the fish and pour off the excess oil, leaving about 1 × 15 ml (1 tablespoon) in the pan. Add the garlic, ginger root and spring onions to the pan and fry for a few seconds only.
Return the carp to the pan, then add the soy sauce, sherry, sugar and stock or water and simmer for 10 to 15 minutes. Mix the cornflour with a little cold water, and add to the pan, stirring constantly. Serve immediately with sesame seed oil as a garnish.

Braised prawns in shells

Metric
225 g Pacific prawns
3 slices ginger root, peeled
1 spring onion
3×15 ml spoons oil

Sauce:
2×15 ml spoons soy sauce
2×15 ml spoons sherry
1×2.5 ml spoon salt
1×5 ml spoon sugar
1×5 ml spoon cornflour
1×5 ml spoon cold water

Imperial
8 oz Pacific prawns
3 slices ginger root, peeled
1 spring onion
3 tablespoons oil

Sauce:
2 tablespoons soy sauce
2 tablespoons sherry
½ teaspoon salt
1 teaspoon sugar
1 teaspoon cornflour
1 teaspoon cold water

Preparation time: about 15 minutes

The best way to eat this is by taking a bite off the prawns, shells and all; suck the sauce in your mouth and at the same time extract the meat off its shell. Absolutely delicious!

Trim off the whiskers and legs of the prawns but leave on the shells. Thinly shred the ginger root and cut the spring onion into short lengths.
In a frying pan or wok heat the oil until hot, then add the ginger root, spring onion and prawns and stir a few times. Combine the sauce ingredients and add to the pan. Blend well, cook for no more than 5 minutes or until the sauce is almost completely evaporated.

Soy fish steak

Metric
450 g fish steak (cod or halibut)
1×2.5 ml spoon salt
2×15 ml spoons sherry
4×15 ml spoons cornflour
1 egg white
1 slice ginger root, peeled
3×15 ml spoons oil
2×15 ml spoons soy sauce
2×5 ml spoons sugar
120 ml Stock (page 13) or water
Chinese parsley, chopped, to garnish

Imperial
1 lb fish steak (cod or halibut)
½ teaspoon salt
2 tablespoons sherry
4 tablespoons cornflour
1 egg white
1 slice ginger root, peeled
3 tablespoons oil
2 tablespoons soy sauce
2 teaspoons sugar
4 fl oz Stock (page 13) or water
Chinese parsley, chopped, to garnish

Preparation time: about 15 minutes

Cut the fish steak into pieces about the size of a matchbox. Mix together the salt, sherry and 1×15 ml spoon (1 tablespoon) of the cornflour then marinate the fish in it for about 30 minutes. Dip the pieces in egg white before coating them with the remaining cornflour. Finely chop the ginger root.
In a frying pan or wok heat the oil until hot, then fry the fish pieces until golden, stirring very gently to separate each piece. Add the ginger root, soy sauce, sugar and stock or water, then cook for about 3 or 4 minutes or until the juice is entirely evaporated. Serve garnished with Chinese parsley.

Braised carp; Braised prawns in shells; Soy fish steak

Squid and green peppers

Metric	Imperial
225 g squid	8 oz squid
100 g green peppers, cored and seeded	4 oz green peppers, cored and seeded
2 slices ginger root, peeled	2 slices ginger root, peeled
oil for deep frying	oil for deep frying
1×5 ml spoon salt	1 teaspoon salt
1×15 ml spoon soy sauce	1 tablespoon soy sauce
1×5 ml spoon vinegar	1 teaspoon vinegar
freshly ground black pepper	freshly ground black pepper
1×5 ml spoon sesame seed oil	1 teaspoon sesame seed oil

Preparation time: 20 minutes

Clean the squid, discarding the head and transparent backbone as well as the ink bag. Peel off the thin skin and cut the flesh into small pieces the size of a matchbox. Slice the green peppers and thinly shred the ginger root.

In a frying pan or wok heat the oil until fairly hot, then deep-fry the squid for about 30 seconds. Pour off the excess oil, leaving about 1×15 ml spoon (1 tablespoon) oil in the pan, add the ginger root and green peppers followed by the squid. Stir a few times, then add the salt, soy sauce, vinegar and pepper, cook for about 1 minute, add the sesame seed oil and serve.

Ginger and spring onion crab

Metric	Imperial
1×750 g crab	1×1-1¾ lb crab
2×15 ml spoons sherry	2 tablespoons sherry
1×15 ml spoon Stock (page 13) or water	1 tablespoon Stock (page 13) or water
2×15 ml spoons cornflour	2 tablespoons cornflour
4 slices ginger root, peeled	4 slices ginger root, peeled
4 spring onions	4 spring onions
3×15 ml spoons oil	3 tablespoons oil
1×5 ml spoon salt	1 teaspoon salt
1×15 ml spoon soy sauce	1 tablespoon soy sauce
2×5 ml spoons sugar	2 teaspoons sugar

Preparation time: 25 to 30 minutes

Break off the legs and crack the claws of the crabs. Wash any mud off the shell and discard the feathery gills and the sac. Crack the shell using a chopper or heavy knife. Marinate all the crab in about 1×15 ml spoon (1 tablespoon) of the sherry and the stock or water, mixed with the cornflour.

Finely chop the ginger root and spring onion together. In a frying pan or wok heat the oil until hot, then fry the crab pieces for about 1 minute. Add the ginger root, spring onions, salt, soy sauce, sugar and the remaining sherry. Cook for about 5 minutes, stirring all the time and add a little water if the mixture becomes very dry.

Squid and green peppers

Fried prawns in batter

Metric
225 g Pacific prawns
1 egg (size 6)
1×2.5 ml spoon salt
3×15 ml spoons plain flour
2×15 ml spoons water
600 ml oil

Dip:
salt and freshly ground
  black pepper or crushed
  sesame seeds, mixed
  together

Imperial
8 oz Pacific prawns
1 egg (small)
½ teaspoon salt
3 tablespoons plain flour
2 tablespoons water
1 pint oil

Dip:
salt and freshly ground
  black pepper or crushed
  sesame seeds, mixed
  together

Preparation time: about 15 minutes

Shell the prawns but leave the tail on to be used as a handle. Make the batter by beating the egg first, then fold in the salt, flour and water. Beat for 1 minute to incorporate some air.

Heat the oil in a deep fryer until really hot, dip each prawn in the batter then deep fry individually for 2 minutes or until golden, remove and drain on kitchen paper. Serve with salt and pepper or crushed sesame seeds as a dip.

Ginger and spring onion crab; Fried prawns in batter

Fish slices in chilli sauce

Metric	Imperial
450 g fish fillet (cod or plaice)	1 lb fish fillet (cod or plaice)
1×15 ml spoon plain flour	1 tablespoon plain flour
300 ml oil	½ pint oil

Sauce:	Sauce:
½×15 ml spoon peeled and finely chopped ginger root	½ tablespoon peeled and finely chopped ginger root
1×15 ml spoon finely chopped spring onion	1 tablespoon finely chopped spring onion
3×15 ml spoons sherry	3 tablespoons sherry
1×15 ml spoon soy sauce	1 tablespoon soy sauce
2×5 ml spoons sugar	2 teaspoons sugar
1×5 ml spoon salt	1 teaspoon salt
1×5 ml spoon vinegar	1 teaspoon vinegar
1-2×15 ml spoons chilli purée	1-2 tablespoons chilli purée

Prawns and green peas

Metric	Imperial
225 g peeled prawns	8 oz peeled prawns
1 egg white	1 egg white
1×15 ml spoon cornflour	1 tablespoon cornflour
1 slice ginger root, peeled	1 slice ginger root, peeled
1 spring onion	1 spring onion
3×15 ml spoons oil	3 tablespoons oil
175 g green peas	6 oz green peas
1½×5 ml spoons salt	1½ teaspoons salt
2×5 ml spoons sugar	2 teaspoons sugar
1×15 ml spoon sherry	1 tablespoon sherry
1×5 ml spoon sesame seed oil	1 teaspoon sesame seed oil

Preparation time: about 15 minutes

Mix the egg white and the cornflour, and coat the prawns with this mixture. Refrigerate the mixture for 20 to 30 minutes.
Finely chop the ginger root and spring onion. Heat the oil in a frying pan or wok and stir-fry the prawns for one minute, then remove and drain them on kitchen paper.
Heat the oil remaining in the pan until hot, toss in the ginger root and spring onion, followed by the green peas; add the prawns, salt, sugar and sherry, stir constantly for about 1 minute, then add the sesame seed oil just before serving.

Preparation time: about 15 minutes

Chilli sauce may be used instead of chilli purée, but reduce the amount by at least a half as it is hotter.

Cut the fillets into small 5 cm (2 inch) slices, then coat them with the flour. Heat the oil in a large frying pan or wok until hot, then fry the fish for 3 minutes. Remove the fish slices, allow the oil to become hot again then return the slices to the pan in order to crisp them. Remove and drain the fish.
Pour off the excess oil from the pan, leaving about 1×15 ml spoon (1 tablespoon). Combine the sauce ingredients and add to the pan with the fish slices. Stir well and simmer for 1 minute before serving.

Sweet and sour fish

Metric	Imperial
1 × 750 g fish (carp, perch, bass or grey mullet)	1 × 1½ lb fish (carp, perch, bass or grey mullet)
1 × 5 ml spoon salt	1 teaspoon salt
2 × 15 ml spoons plain flour	2 tablespoons plain flour
300 ml oil	½ pint oil

Sauce:	Sauce:
3 × 15 ml spoons Stock (page 13) or water	3 tablespoons Stock (page 13) or water
2 × 15 ml spoons sugar	2 tablespoons sugar
2 × 15 ml spoons wine vinegar	2 tablespoons wine vinegar
1 × 15 ml spoon soy sauce	1 tablespoon soy sauce
2 × 5 ml spoons cornflour	2 teaspoons cornflour

Preparation time: about 15 minutes

Scale and clean the fish if it has not already been done. Slash both sides of the skin diagonally as far as the bone at intervals of 1 cm (½ inch). Dry it thoroughly and rub on the salt both inside and out, then coat the fish with the flour.
In a frying pan or wok, heat the oil until hot, then fry the fish for 4 to 5 minutes or until golden brown, turning it once. Remove the fish and place it on a serving dish. Combine the sauce ingredients. Pour off the excess oil from the pan, add the sauce mixture, stir and simmer until thickened, then pour it all over the fish and serve at once.

Fish slices in chilli sauce; Prawns and green peas;
Sweet and sour fish

Prawns fu-yung

Metric	Imperial
100 g prawns	*4 oz prawns*
1 slice ginger root, peeled	*1 slice ginger root, peeled*
1×5 ml spoon cornflour	*1 teaspoon cornflour*
6 eggs	*6 eggs*
1×5 ml spoon salt	*1 teaspoon salt*
1 spring onion, finely chopped	*1 spring onion, finely chopped*
3×15 ml spoons oil	*3 tablespoons oil*
1×15 ml spoon sherry	*1 tablespoon sherry*

Preparation time: about 20 minutes

Wash and shell the prawns, then dry them well on kitchen paper. Finely chop the ginger root and mix it with the prawns and cornflour. Beat the eggs with the salt and the finely chopped spring onion.
In a frying pan or wok heat 1×15 ml spoon (1 tablespoon) of the oil, and before it gets too hot, stir-fry the prawns, add the sherry, then remove the prawns from the pan and mix with the eggs.
Clean the pan, heat the remaining oil in it, then pour in the eggs. Stir to scramble for a few minutes and serve before the eggs set too hard.

Prawns fu-yung; Fried prawn balls; Fried fish slices

Fried prawn balls

Metric	Imperial
450 g uncooked prawns	*1 lb uncooked prawns*
50 g pork fat	*2 oz pork fat*
4 water chestnuts, peeled	*4 water chestnuts, peeled*
1 egg white	*1 egg white*
2×15 ml spoons cornflour	*2 tablespoons cornflour*
1×5 ml spoon salt	*1 teaspoon salt*
1×15 ml spoon sherry	*1 tablespoon sherry*
freshly ground black pepper	*freshly ground black pepper*
oil for deep frying	*oil for deep frying*

Preparation time: about 30 minutes

You can use crab meat or white fish fillets instead of prawns.

Shell the prawns, finely chop them with the pork fat and water chestnuts. Mix with all the other ingredients and leave to stand for 30 minutes.
In a frying pan or wok heat the oil until hot.
Using a teaspoon, scoop up a spoonful of prawn mixture at a time, roughly in the shape of a ball, and lower it into the hot oil. Fry the prawn balls until golden brown, then remove and drain them on kitchen paper. They should be crisp outside and tender inside.

Fried fish slices

Metric	*Imperial*
450 g fish fillet (plaice or sole)	*1 lb fish fillet (plaice or sole)*
1 × 15 ml spoon sherry	*1 tablespoon sherry*
1 egg white	*1 egg white*
1 × 15 ml spoon cornflour	*1 tablespoon cornflour*
1 garlic clove	*1 garlic clove*
1 spring onion	*1 spring onion*
1 slice ginger root, peeled	*1 slice ginger root, peeled*
¼ red pepper	*¼ red pepper*
300 ml oil	*½ pint oil*

Sauce:	*Sauce:*
120 ml Stock (page 13)	*4 fl oz Stock (page 13)*
2 × 5 ml spoons salt	*2 teaspoons salt*
1 × 5 ml spoon sugar	*1 teaspoon sugar*
2 × 5 ml spoons cornflour	*2 teaspoons cornflour*
1 × 5 ml spoon sesame seed oil	*1 teaspoon sesame seed oil*

Preparation time: about 20 minutes

Cut the fish into thin 5 cm (2 inch) slices. Mix together the sherry, egg white and cornflour, then marinate the fish in it for about 20 minutes. Finely chop the garlic and spring onion, thinly shred the ginger root and red pepper.

In a frying pan or wok, heat the oil until hot, then fry the fish slices for 2 to 3 minutes or until golden. Remove and drain the fish on kitchen paper. Pour off the excess oil from the pan, then add the garlic, spring onion, ginger root and red pepper.

Blend together the sauce ingredients, add to the pan with the fish, stir over the heat and serve.

29

POULTRY

In China, chicken is regarded as both a festive dish, as well as for everyday meals, while duck is only eaten on special occasions. Chicken is very versatile as it can be cooked in so many different ways; it can be combined with almost any other ingredient and yet it will retain its characteristic texture and flavour.

As the Chinese use only chopsticks at the table, a chicken or duck has to be served cut into small pieces even if it is cooked whole. To do this you will need a sharp cleaver in order to cut through the bone.
1. Remove the two legs by breaking the joints.
2. Cut the body into two halves lengthwise.
3. Remove the two breasts from the backbone.
4. Remove the two wings by breaking the joints.
5. Cut each of the eight parts into 3 to 4 pieces, then reassemble the pieces neatly on a serving dish.

Peking duck

Metric
1×2 kg duckling
*1×15 ml spoon brown
    sugar*
1×5 ml spoon salt
300 ml warm water

Pancakes:
450 g plain flour
300 ml boiling water
1×15 ml spoon oil
10 spring onions
½ cucumber
*6×15 ml spoons Hoi sin
    sauce*

Imperial
1×4½-4¾ lb duckling
*1 tablespoon brown
    sugar*
1 teaspoon salt
½ pint warm water

Pancakes:
1 lb plain flour
½ pint boiling water
1 tablespoon oil
10 spring onions
½ cucumber
*6 tablespoons Hoi sin
    sauce*

Preparation time: about 6 hours

Oven: 200°C, 400°F, Gas Mark 6

The actual cooking of this famous dish is very simple, but the preparation and serving require some special care. While the duck is roasting some thin pancakes are made, in which the duck pieces are traditionally served. The carcass of the duck can be used to make stock or a good soup with vegetables.

Clean the duck well then hang it up to dry thoroughly overnight in a draught.
Dissolve the sugar and salt in the warm water and rub all over the duck with this mixture. Then hang it up to dry thoroughly once more.
To cook, place the duck on the middle shelf of a preheated oven, with the dish of water below to catch the fat. Roast the duck for 1¼ hours. There is nothing to be done while the duck is being cooked, no basting nor turning over so you can take this opportunity to cook the pancakes which are served with the duck.
Sift the flour into a mixing bowl and very carefully pour in the boiling water mixed with 1×5 ml spoon (1 teaspoon) of the oil, stirring as you pour.
Knead the mixture into a firm dough, then divide it into 3 equal portions. Roll out each portion into a long 'sausage', and cut each 'sausage' into 8 equal pieces. Using the palm of your hand, press each piece into a flat pancake. Brush one of the pancakes with a little oil, and place another on top to form a 'sandwich', so that you end up with 12 'sandwiches'. Using a rolling pin, flatten each sandwich into a 15 cm (6 inch) circle, rolling each side gently on a lightly floured surface.
Place an ungreased frying pan over a high heat. When it is hot, reduce the heat to moderate and put one pancake 'sandwich' at a time into the pan, turn it over when it starts to puff up with air bubbles. When little brown spots appear on the underside, remove it from the pan and very gently peel apart the two layers. Keep the pancakes under a damp cloth to prevent them drying out. Fold each in half for serving.
Cut the spring onions into 5 cm (2 inch) lengths and slice the cucumber into thin strips about the same size as the spring onions.
The duck is carved at the table, with the skin and meat served in separate dishes.
To eat, spread a pancake with a little Hoi sin sauce. Place a few spring onions and cucumber strips in the middle and top with a piece or two of duck meat and the crispy skin. Roll up the pancake like a sausage roll, turning up the bottom end to prevent anything dropping out.

Peking duck

Diced chicken with peppers

Metric
225 g chicken breast meat, boned and skinned
1×2.5 ml spoon salt
1 egg white
1×15 ml spoon cornflour
1 green pepper, cored and seeded
1 red pepper, cored and seeded
2 slices ginger root, peeled
2 spring onions
2 chillis, seeded
4×15 ml spoons oil
2×15 ml spoons crushed black bean sauce

Imperial
8 oz chicken breast meat, boned and skinned
½ teaspoon salt
1 egg white
1 tablespoon cornflour
1 green pepper, cored and seeded
1 red pepper, cored and seeded
2 slices ginger root, peeled
2 spring onions
2 chillis, seeded
4 tablespoons oil
2 tablespoons crushed black bean sauce

Preparation time: 25 minutes

This is a very colourful dish with a piquant flavour. The meat should be tender and the peppers crisp and crunchy.

Cut the chicken meat into little cubes. Mix the cubes with first the salt, then the egg white and finally the cornflour. It is very important that they are mixed in that order.

Cut the green and red peppers into small square pieces the same size as the chicken cubes. Cut the ginger root, spring onions and chillis into slivers.

Heat the oil in a wok or frying pan and stir-fry the chicken over a moderate heat, separating the cubes. Cook until the cubes are lightly coloured, then remove them with a perforated spoon.

Increase the heat, and when the oil is really hot, put in the ginger root, spring onions and hot chillis, stir a few times then add the green and red peppers. Continue stirring for about 30 seconds, then add the black bean sauce and the chicken cubes, stirring well for about 1 to 1½ minutes. Serve hot.

Braised duck; Diced chicken with peppers

Chicken salad

Braised duck

Metric	Imperial
2.5 litres water	4½ pints water
1 × 2.25-2.5 kg duckling	1 × 5-5¼ lb duckling
3 spring onions	3 spring onions
5 × 15 ml spoons soy sauce	5 tablespoons soy sauce
3 × 15 ml spoons sherry	3 tablespoons sherry
1 × 15 ml spoon brandy	1 tablespoon brandy
3 × 15 ml spoons candy sugar or coffee sugar crystals	3 tablespoons candy sugar or coffee sugar crystals

Preparation time: 5 to 10 minutes

Bring the water to the boil in a large saucepan or casserole, put in the duck and boil rapidly for 4 to 5 minutes, turning it over once or twice. Discard two-thirds of the water, then add the spring onions, soy sauce, sherry and brandy.

Bring the water back to the boil, then cover tightly and simmer gently for 30 minutes, turning the duck over at least once. Add the candy sugar and continue cooking for a further 1 to 1½ hours.

Either serve the duck whole in its own juice, or take it out and cut it into small pieces (see page 30) and arrange them neatly on a plate. Serve hot the European way with rice or pasta as an accompaniment, or cold with a salad.

Serves 4.

Chicken salad

Metric	Imperial
450 g cooked chicken meat	1 lb cooked chicken meat
1 small cucumber	1 small cucumber
50 g ginger root, peeled	2 oz ginger root, peeled
4 spring onions (white parts only)	4 spring onions (white parts only)
Dressing:	**Dressing:**
1½ × 5 ml spoons salt	1½ teaspoons salt
1 × 15 ml spoon sugar	1 tablespoon sugar
1 × 15 ml spoon lemon juice	1 tablespoon lemon juice
1–2 × 5 ml spoons chilli sauce	1–2 teaspoons chilli sauce
1 × 15 ml spoon sesame seed oil	1 tablespoon sesame seed oil
finely chopped fresh parsley, to garnish	finely chopped fresh parsley, to garnish

Preparation time: 20 to 25 minutes

Chilli sauce is very hot, so use it cautiously according to your taste.

Remove any bones and skin from the chicken meat, then cut the meat into fine shreds the size of a matchstick. Cut the cucumber, ginger root and spring onions into thin shreds also, then place them with the chicken meat in a large bowl or deep dish.

Mix together the ingredients for the dressing and pour it over the chicken mixture, toss well and let it stand for 1 hour before serving.

Shredded chicken and celery

Metric	*Imperial*
225 g chicken breast meat, boned and skinned	8 oz chicken breast meat, boned and skinned
1 × 2.5 ml spoon salt	½ teaspoon salt
1 egg white	1 egg white
1 × 15 ml spoon cornflour	1 tablespoon cornflour
1 small celery stick	1 small celery stick
1 green pepper	1 green pepper
4 slices ginger root, peeled	4 slices ginger root, peeled
2 spring onions	2 spring onions
4 × 15 ml spoons oil	4 tablespoons oil
2 × 15 ml spoons soy sauce	2 tablespoons soy sauce
1 × 15 ml spoon sherry	1 tablespoon sherry

Preparation time: 25 to 30 minutes

For the best flavour use a young chicken (not a boiler), and because of the cooking method the chicken must not have been frozen. It may seem surprising that the chicken is simmered for only 15 minutes, but it does, in fact, continue to cook in the hot water until deliciously tender.

Cut the celery, green pepper, ginger root and spring onions into slivers the same size as the chicken.
Heat the oil in a wok or frying pan and stir-fry the chicken shreds over moderate heat until the pieces are lightly coloured. Remove the chicken with a perforated spoon.
Increase the heat, and when the oil is very hot, put in the ginger root and spring onions followed by the celery and green pepper. Stir continuously for about 30 seconds, then add the chicken shreds with the soy sauce and sherry. Blend well and cook for a further 1 to 1½ minutes, stirring. Serve hot.

Boiled chicken

Metric	Imperial
1×1.25 kg fresh chicken	*1×2½–2¾ lb fresh chicken*
2 slices ginger root	*2 slices ginger root*
2 spring onions	*2 spring onions*
1×5 ml spoon salt	*1 teaspoon salt*
1×15 ml spoon finely chopped spring onion, to garnish	*1 tablespoon finely chopped spring onion, to garnish*

Sauce:	*Sauce:*
2×15 ml spoons soy sauce	*2 tablespoons soy sauce*
1×15 ml spoon sesame seed oil	*1 tablespoon sesame seed oil*

Preparation time: 15 minutes

For the best flavour use a young chicken (not a boiler) that has not been frozen. It may seem surprising that the chicken is simmered for only 15 minutes, but it does, in fact, continue to cook in the hot water until deliciously tender.

Clean the chicken well, place it in a saucepan and cover with cold water. Add the ginger root, spring onions and salt. Bring to the boil, then cover and simmer very gently for 15 minutes. Keep the pan covered and leave the bird to cool in the water for at least 2 to 3 hours or until needed.
To serve, take the chicken out of the pan and cut it into small pieces (see page 30). Arrange the pieces neatly on a dish and garnish with the finely chopped spring onion. Mix together the soy sauce and sesame seed oil, then either pour the sauce mixture over it or serve the sauce as a dip in individual saucers on the table.

Shredded chicken and celery; Boiled chicken

Drunken chicken

Metric
1 × 1.5 kg chicken
2 × 5 ml spoons salt
2 slices ginger root
4 spring onions
1.75 litres water
finely chopped fresh
    parsley, to garnish

Sauce:
2 × 15 ml spoons soy sauce
1 × 15 ml spoon brown
    sugar
300 ml sherry
1 × 15 ml spoon brandy

Imperial
1 × 3–3½ lb chicken
2 teaspoons salt
2 slices ginger root
4 spring onions
3 pints water
finely chopped fresh
    parsley, to garnish

Sauce:
2 tablespoons soy sauce
1 tablespoon brown
    sugar
½ pint sherry
1 tablespoon brandy

As for Boiled Chicken (page 35) use only fresh chicken.

Preparation time: about 30 minutes

Rub the chicken with a little of the salt and leave it to stand for about 20 minutes. Place the remaining salt, ginger root, spring onions and water in a saucepan or flameproof casserole and bring to the boil. Add the chicken, cover and bring to the boil, then reduce the heat and cook for 15 minutes. Bring to a rapid boil, turn off the heat and leave to cool in the water for at least 2 to 3 hours before taking out the bird.

Cut the chicken into small pieces (see page 30), arrange it neatly in a deep dish with the skin-side down. Place all the sauce ingredients in a pan and bring to the boil, stirring to dissolve the sugar. Immediately pour the sauce over the chicken then cover and place in the refrigerator for 2 to 3 hours.

Serve the chicken skin-side up, sprinkled with parsley.

Drunken chicken; Chicken and bean-sprouts

Soy chicken with Celery salad

Chicken and bean-sprouts

Metric	*Imperial*
225 g chicken breast meat, boned and skinned	8 oz chicken breast meat, boned and skinned
2 × 5 ml spoons salt	2 teaspoons salt
1 egg white	1 egg white
1 × 15 ml spoon cornflour	1 tablespoon cornflour
225 g fresh bean-sprouts	8 oz fresh bean-sprouts
1 small red pepper	1 small red pepper
4 × 15 ml spoons oil	4 tablespoons oil
2 × 15 ml spoons Stock (page 13)	2 tablespoons Stock (page 13)

Preparation time: 25 to 30 minutes

Slice the chicken meat into slivers not much bigger than a matchstick. Mix the slivers with 1 × 2.5 ml spoon (½ teaspoon) of the salt, then the egg white and finally the cornflour, in that order.

Wash the bean-sprouts in a basin of cold water, discarding the husks and any little bits that float to the surface (it is not necessary to top and tail each sprout, that would be too time consuming). Cut the red pepper into thin shreds.

Heat the oil in a wok or frying pan and stir-fry the chicken pieces until lightly coloured, then remove them with a perforated spoon.

Increase the heat and when the oil is hot, add the bean-sprouts and red pepper followed by the chicken. Stir a few times, then add the remaining salt and the stock. Cook for about 1 minute more. Serve hot or cold.

Soy chicken

Metric	*Imperial*
1 × 1.5 kg chicken	1 × 3-3½ lb chicken
2 × 15 ml spoons crushed yellow bean sauce	2 tablespoons crushed yellow bean sauce
1 × 2.5 ml spoon five-spice powder	½ teaspoon five-spice powder
2 × 15 ml spoons water	2 tablespoons water
2 slices ginger root	2 slices ginger root
2 spring onions	2 spring onions
4 × 15 ml spoons soy sauce	4 tablespoons soy sauce
2 × 15 ml spoons sherry	2 tablespoons sherry
450 ml Stock (page 13) or water	¾ pint Stock (page 13) or water

Preparation time: 25 to 30 minutes

This sauce will keep in the refrigerator for up to 6 to 8 weeks if boiled up once a week, and can be re-used for other recipes.

Clean the chicken well. Mix the crushed bean sauce and five-spice powder with the water, then pour the mixture into the cavity of the chicken.

Place the chicken in a saucepan or flameproof casserole dish and add the remaining ingredients. Simmer gently for about 1½ hours, turning the bird over several times during cooking and basting it frequently with the sauce.

Remove the chicken from the pan and leave it to cool before cutting into small pieces (see page 30). Serve cold on a bed of lettuce and with a Celery Salad (page 58).

Chicken and mushrooms

Metric	Imperial
225 g chicken breast meat, boned and skinned	8 oz chicken breast meat, boned and skinned
1 egg white	1 egg white
2×5 ml spoons cornflour	2 teaspoons cornflour
1½×5 ml spoons salt	1½ teaspoons salt
225 g fresh mushrooms	8 oz fresh mushrooms
100 g water chestnuts	4 oz water chestnuts
100 g peas	4 oz peas
2 spring onions	2 spring onions
4×15 ml spoons oil	4 tablespoons oil
1×15 ml spoon soy sauce	1 tablespoon soy sauce
1×5 ml spoon sugar	1 teaspoon sugar

Preparation time: 15 to 20 minutes

Cut the chicken breast meat into thin slices about the size of an oblong postage stamp. Mix the slices with the egg white blended with cornflour and 1×2.5 ml spoon (½ teaspoon) of the salt.
Thinly slice the mushrooms and water chestnuts. Cut the spring onions into short lengths.
Heat about half the oil in a wok or frying pan, but do not allow it to get too hot. Stir-fry the chicken slices until lightly coloured, then remove with a perforated spoon.
Heat the remaining oil in the wok until smoking, toss in the spring onions followed by the mushrooms, water chestnuts and peas, add the remaining salt and stir for a while. Add the chicken slices together with the soy sauce and sugar. Cook together for about 1 minute. Serve hot.

Diced chicken with crushed peanuts

Metric	Imperial
225 g chicken breast meat, skinned and boned	8 oz chicken breast meat, skinned and boned
1×2.5 ml spoon salt	½ teaspoon salt
1 egg white	1 egg white
2×5 ml spoons cornflour	2 teaspoons cornflour
50 g roasted peanuts, shelled	2 oz roasted peanuts, shelled
2 spring onions	2 spring onions
3 dried red chillis, soaked	3 dried red chillis, soaked
3×15 ml spoons oil	3 tablespoons oil

Sauce:	Sauce:
1×15 ml spoon sugar	1 tablespoon sugar
1×15 ml spoon vinegar	1 tablespoon vinegar
1½×5 ml spoons cornflour	1½ teaspoons cornflour
1×15 ml spoon water	1 tablespoon water

Preparation time: 15 to 20 minutes

Dice the chicken into small cubes not much bigger than the size of a peanut. Mix the cubes with salt, egg white and cornflour.
Crush or finely chop the peanuts. Cut the spring onions into short lengths. Finely chop the soaked red chillis. Mix the sauce ingredients together in a bowl or jug.
Heat the oil in a wok or frying pan and stir-fry the chicken until lightly coloured, then remove with a perforated spoon. Toss the spring onions and red chillis into the wok, stir a few times, add the crushed peanuts, diced chicken and the sauce mixture, blend well.
Serve as soon as the sauce thickens.

Walnut chicken

Metric
275 g chicken breast meat,
  skinned and boned
1 ×5 ml spoon salt
1 ×15 ml spoon sherry
2 egg whites
4 ×15 ml spoons cornflour
100 g walnuts, coarsely
  chopped
1 litre oil for deep-frying
½ cucumber, sliced, to
  garnish

Imperial
10 oz chicken breast meat,
  skinned and boned
1 teaspoon salt
1 tablespoon sherry
2 egg whites
4 tablespoons cornflour
4 oz walnuts, coarsely
  chopped
1¾ pints oil for deep-frying
½ cucumber, sliced, to
  garnish

Preparation time: 20 to 25 minutes

Cut the chicken breast meat into small pieces about
the size of a matchbox. Marinate the pieces in the
salt mixed with the sherry for about 20 minutes.
Lightly beat the egg whites, fold in the cornflour
and mix well.
Dip the chicken pieces in the egg-white mixture and
roll each piece in the chopped walnuts.
Heat the oil in a wok or saucepan until fairly hot and
deep-fry the chicken pieces one by one until golden.
Remove with a perforated spoon and drain.
Serve garnished with cucumber slices.

Diced chicken with crushed peanuts; Chicken and mushrooms;
Walnut chicken

MEAT

Undoubtedly, the most popular meat eaten in China is pork. In everyday terms, the Chinese words for 'pork' and 'meat' are synonymous, except for a small percentage of the population: the Chinese Moslems, Mongols, Manchus and the inhabitants of Xinjiang (Sinkiang), totalling about 10 million people, whose principal meat consists of beef, lamb or mutton.

Like chicken, pork is most versatile, and adapts itself to a wide range of different cooking methods. Pork can also be combined with a limitless amount of other ingredients. In many recipes, pork and chicken are almost interchangeable with other meat.

Barbecued pork spare ribs

Metric	Imperial
750 g pork spare ribs	1½ lb pork spare ribs

Hoi Sin Sauce:
3×15 ml spoons crushed yellow bean sauce	3 tablespoons crushed yellow bean sauce
1×15 ml spoon plain flour	1 tablespoon plain flour
1×15 ml spoon sugar	1 tablespoon sugar
2×15 ml spoons vinegar	2 tablespoons vinegar
1×5 ml spoon chilli sauce	1 teaspoon chilli sauce
1×5 ml spoon sesame seed oil	1 teaspoon sesame seed oil
1 garlic clove, crushed	1 garlic clove, crushed
2×15 ml spoons sherry	2 tablespoons sherry

Preparation time: 10 minutes

Oven: 220°C, 425°F, Gas Mark 7

Commercially made Hoi sin sauce is available from Chinese food shops. However, you can make your own sauce quite simply as in this recipe.

Chop the spare ribs into small pieces. Marinate them in 4×15 ml spoons (4 tablespoons) homemade or commercial Hoi sin sauce and the sherry for at least 1 hour, turning over once or twice.
Cook the ribs on a barbecue grid for about 10 minutes, turning them once or twice. Alternatively place them on a baking tray and roast in a preheated oven for 15 to 20 minutes until brown.
Serve with Fried Rice (page 68) and a vegetable dish such as Fried Lettuce (page 59).

Barbecued pork spare ribs; Sweet and sour deep-fried pork

Sweet and sour deep-fried pork

Metric	Imperial
225 g pork, not too lean	8 oz pork, not too lean
100 g bamboo shoots	4 oz bamboo shoots
1 green pepper, cored and seeded	1 green pepper, cored and seeded
1 spring onion	1 spring onion
1×5 ml spoon salt	1 teaspoon salt
1½×15 ml spoons brandy	1½ tablespoons brandy
1 egg	1 egg
1×15 ml spoon cornflour	1 tablespoon cornflour
oil for deep frying	oil for deep frying
3×15 ml spoons plain flour	3 tablespoons plain flour

Sauce:
3×15 ml spoons vinegar	3 tablespoons vinegar
3×15 ml spoons sugar	3 tablespoons sugar
1×2.5 ml spoon salt	½ teaspoon salt
1×15 ml spoon tomato purée	1 tablespoon tomato purée
1×15 ml spoon soy sauce	1 tablespoon soy sauce
1×15 ml spoon cornflour	1 tablespoon cornflour
1×5 ml spoon sesame seed oil	1 teaspoon sesame seed oil

Preparation time: 20 to 25 minutes

Cut the pork into about 24 small cubes. Cut the bamboo shoots and green pepper into small pieces of the same size. Then cut the spring onion into 2.5 cm (1 inch) lengths.
Mix the pork with the salt and brandy and marinate for 15 minutes. Add a beaten egg and the cornflour and blend well.
Mix together the sauce ingredients.
Heat the oil in a wok or saucepan. Coat each piece of meat with the flour and deep fry for three minutes, then remove the wok or saucepan from the heat but leave the meat in the oil for a further 2 minutes before removing with a perforated spoon. Heat the oil again. Re-fry the meat with the bamboo shoots for 2 minutes or until they are golden, then remove and drain.
Pour off the excess oil, leaving about 1×15 ml spoon (1 tablespoon) in the wok or frying pan. Add the spring onion and the green pepper followed by the sweet and sour sauce mixture and stir until it thickens, and there is not much sauce left. Add the pork and the bamboo shoots, blend well and serve hot.

Pork and mixed vegetables (chop suey)

Metric	Imperial
225 g pork fillet, chicken meat or beef steak	8 oz pork fillet, chicken meat or beef steak
2×15 ml spoons soy sauce	2 tablespoons soy sauce
1×15 ml spoon sherry	1 tablespoon sherry
2×5 ml spoons cornflour	2 teaspoons cornflour
100 g fresh bean-sprouts	4 oz fresh bean-sprouts
2 spring onions	2 spring onions
1 slice ginger root, peeled	1 slice ginger root, peeled
1 small green pepper, cored and seeded	1 small green pepper, cored and seeded
a few cauliflower or broccoli florets	a few cauliflower or broccoli florets
2-3 tomatoes	2-3 tomatoes
1-2 carrots, peeled	1-2 carrots, peeled
50 g green beans	2 oz green beans
5×15 ml spoons oil	5 tablespoons oil
2×5 ml spoons salt	2 teaspoons salt
1×15 ml spoon sugar	1 tablespoon sugar
3×15 ml spoons Stock (page 13) or water	3 tablespoons Stock (page 13) or water

Preparation time: 20 to 25 minutes

This is a basic recipe for cooking pork, chicken, beef or prawns with vegetables (usually several different kinds, which can be varied according to seasonal availability). It is also regarded as an excellent way of using a few leftover vegetables.

Cut the meat into small slices not much bigger than a postage stamp. Mix together the soy sauce, sherry and cornflour, and stir in the meat until each slice is coated with mixture.
Cut the spring onions into 2.5 cm (1 inch) lengths and finely chop the ginger root.
Wash the bean-sprouts in a basin of cold water, discarding the husks and any little bits that float to the surface of the water.
Cut the green pepper, cauliflower or broccoli, tomatoes, carrots and green beans into small pieces.
Heat about half the oil in a wok or frying pan and stir-fry the meat slices for about 1 minute, stirring constantly, then remove with a perforated spoon and put them on one side.
Heat the remaining oil, add the spring onions and ginger root, followed by the rest of the vegetables and the salt and sugar. Stir for about 1 minute and add the meat. Blend everything well and moisten with a little stock or water if necessary.
Serve with boiled rice.

Pork and mixed vegetables (chop suey)

Roast crispy pork

Metric	Imperial
1 kg belly of pork	2-2¼ lb belly of pork
2×5 ml spoons salt	2 teaspoons salt
1×5 ml spoon five-spice powder	1 teaspoon five-spice powder
Dip:	**Dip:**
4×15 ml spoons soy sauce	4 tablespoons soy sauce

Preparation time: 10 minutes

Oven: 240°C, 475°F, Gas Mark 9 reduced to 200°C, 400°F, Gas Mark 6

Ideally, the pork should be in one piece. Dry the skin well and make sure that it is free from hairs. Mix together the salt and five-spice powder, then rub the mixture all over the meat and leave to stand in a covered dish for about 1 hour.
Place the pork, skin side up, on the middle shelf of a hot oven, with a dish of water below to catch the fat. After 20 minutes reduce the heat to moderate and cook for a further 40 to 45 minutes or until the skin has become crackling. Cut into small slices and serve hot or cold with cold soy sauce as a dip.

From the left: Roast crispy pork; Braised leg of pork with Fried cauliflower in the background

Braised leg of pork

Metric
1 ×1.25-1.5 kg leg of pork
5 ×15 ml spoons soy sauce
50 g candy sugar or coffee
  sugar crystals
4 ×15 ml spoons sherry
1 ×15 ml spoon brandy
2 spring onions
2 slices ginger root, peeled

Imperial
1 ×2½-3½ lb leg of pork
5 tablespoons soy sauce
2 oz candy sugar or coffee
  sugar crystals
4 tablespoons sherry
1 tablespoon brandy
2 spring onions
2 slices ginger root, peeled

Preparation time: 5 to 10 minutes

Like many casseroles, this is even more delicious if cooked in advance and then reheated and served the following day. Any leftovers can be cut into slices and served cold as an excellent starter.

Clean the skin of the pork well and make sure that it is smooth and free of hairs. To prevent the skin from sticking to the pan, score an X mark down the middle as far as the bone.

Place the pork in a large flameproof casserole dish or saucepan with the skin side down. Cover it with cold water and bring it to a rapid boil, skimming off the scum. Add all the other ingredients, cover tightly, reduce the heat and simmer gently for 30 minutes.

Turn the pork over, replace the lid tightly and continue cooking for about 2 hours. The juice will now have reduced to not much more than 150 ml (¼ pint). Turn the heat up for 5 minutes to thicken the gravy, then lift out the pork and place it in a large bowl or a deep dish. Pour the thick gravy over the pork and serve.

Pork in fragrant sauce

Metric	Imperial
1 kg pork belly	2-2¼ lb pork belly
2 spring onions	2 spring onions
2 slices ginger root, peeled	2 slices ginger root, peeled
4×15 ml spoons soy sauce	4 tablespoons soy sauce
3×15 ml spoons sherry	3 tablespoons sherry
1×15 ml spoon brandy	1 tablespoon brandy
2×15 ml spoons sugar	2 tablespoons sugar
2×5 ml spoons five-spice powder	2 teaspoons five-spice powder
1×5 ml spoon salt	1 teaspoon salt
1 lettuce heart, washed	1 lettuce heart, washed

Preparation time: 5 minutes

This sauce can be kept in the refrigerator for up to 4 weeks if boiled up once a week and cooled quickly before refrigerating.

Cut the pork into 3 or 4 chunks, place it in a large saucepan or flameproof casserole dish with the spring onions, ginger root, soy sauce, sherry, brandy, sugar, five-spice powder and salt. Add just enough water to cover the pork. Bring it to the boil, cover and cook over a fairly high heat for about 3 hours, adding a little boiling water now and again to prevent the meat from drying out.
To serve, remove the meat from the sauce, cut it into thin slices like bacon rashers, and serve on a bed of lettuce leaves.

Fried pork liver

Metric	Imperial
225 g pork liver	8 oz pork liver
1×15 ml spoon soy sauce	1 tablespoon soy sauce
1×15 ml spoon cornflour	1 tablespoon cornflour
25 g dried wooden ears (optional)	1 oz dried wooden ears (optional)
100 g onions, peeled	4 oz onions, peeled
4×15 ml spoons oil	4 tablespoons oil
1×5 ml spoon salt	1 teaspoon salt
1×15 ml spoon sherry	1 tablespoon sherry
1×5 ml spoon sugar	1 teaspoon sugar
3×15 ml spoons Stock (page 13) or water	3 tablespoons Stock (page 13) or water
1×5 ml spoon sesame seed oil	1 teaspoon sesame seed oil

Preparation time: 20 minutes

Cut the liver into thickish slices about the size of a match box. Mix together the soy sauce and the cornflour and add the liver.
Soak the wooden ears in warm water for about 15 to 20 minutes, then rinse and discard any hard parts. Thinly slice the onions.
Heat about half the oil in a wok or frying pan until hot and stir-fry the liver for about 20 to 30 seconds, or until all the pieces are separated. Remove with a perforated spoon.
Heat the remaining oil in the pan, and when hot, stir in the onions and wooden ears. Return the liver with the salt, sherry and sugar to the wok. Blend well and add a little stock or water if necessary. Add the sesame seed oil and serve hot.

Fried meat with beans

Metric
225 g pork fillet or frying
steak
2×15 ml spoons soy sauce
1×15 ml spoon cornflour
225 g fresh French beans,
washed, topped and
tailed
4×15 ml spoons oil
1×5 ml spoon salt
1×15 ml spoon sherry
2×15 ml spoons Stock
(page 13) or water

Imperial
8 oz pork fillet or frying
steak
2 tablespoons soy sauce
1 tablespoon cornflour
8 oz fresh French beans,
washed, topped and
tailed
4 tablespoons oil
1 teaspoon salt
1 tablespoon sherry
2 tablespoons Stock
(page 13) or water

Preparation time: 20 to 25 minutes

Cut the meat into thin shreds about the size of a
matchstick. Mix together the soy sauce and cornflour, then marinate the pieces of meat in it for about
10 minutes.
Cut the beans into 5 cm (2 inch) lengths (dwarf beans
can be left whole).
Heat half the oil in a wok or frying pan and stir-fry the
meat for about 1 minute or until lightly coloured, then
remove with a perforated spoon and set aside.
Heat the remaining oil and stir-fry the beans with the
salt for about 1 minute, then add the meat and sherry.
Blend well together and add a little stock or water if
necessary, but do not over cook, otherwise the beans
will lose their crispiness and the meat its tenderness.
Serve hot.

Pork in fragrant sauce; Fried pork liver; Fried meat with beans

Pork with mushrooms and bamboo shoots with Fried rice

Pork with mushrooms and bamboo shoots

Metric
4 Chinese dried mushrooms
225 g pork fillet
2×15 ml spoons soy sauce
1×15 ml spoon cornflour
225 g bamboo shoots
4×15 ml spoons oil
1½×5 ml spoons salt
2×15 ml spoons sherry

Imperial
4 Chinese dried mushrooms
8 oz pork fillet
2 tablespoons soy sauce
1 tablespoon cornflour
8 oz bamboo shoots
4 tablespoons oil
1½ teaspoons salt
2 tablespoons sherry

Preparation time: 25 to 30 minutes

Soak the mushrooms in warm water for about 20 minutes, then squeeze dry and discard the hard stalks. Halve or quarter the mushrooms depending on their size. Retain the soaking liquid.
Cut the pork into thin slices about the size of a large postage stamp. Mix together the soy sauce and the cornflour, then add the pork.
Cut the bamboo shoots into thin slices the same size as the pieces of pork.
Heat about half the oil in a wok or frying pan and stir-fry the pork slices for about 1 minute or until lightly coloured. Remove the pork with a perforated spoon and set aside.
Heat the remaining oil, stir-fry the mushrooms and bamboo shoots, then add the salt, pork and sherry, stirring well. Cook for a further minute or so, stirring constantly and, if necessary, add a little of the water in which the mushrooms have been soaked.
Serve hot.

Pork meat balls with vegetables

Metric	Imperial
450 g pork, not too lean	*1 lb pork, not too lean*
2×15 ml spoons soy sauce	*2 tablespoons soy sauce*
1×15 ml spoon sherry	*1 tablespoon sherry*
1¼×5 ml spoons sugar	*1¼ teaspoons sugar*
1 egg	*1 egg*
1×15 ml spoon cornflour	*1 tablespoon cornflour*
3-4 Chinese dried mushrooms	*3-4 Chinese dried mushrooms*
100 g transparent noodles	*4 oz transparent noodles*
225 g Chinese cabbage or other greens	*8 oz Chinese cabbage or other greens*
2 slices ginger root, peeled	*2 slices ginger root, peeled*
2 spring onions (white parts only)	*2 spring onions (white parts only)*
3×15 ml spoons oil	*3 tablespoons oil*
1×5 ml spoon salt	*1 teaspoon salt*
3×15 ml spoons Stock (page 13) or water	*3 tablespoons Stock (page 13) or water*

Preparation time: 20 to 25 minutes

Finely mince or chop the pork, mix with the soy sauce, sherry, sugar, egg and cornflour. Divide the mixture into 12, flour your hands, and roll the mixture into balls. Refrigerate until needed.

Soak the mushrooms in warm water for about 20 minutes, then squeeze dry and discard the hard stalks. Soak the transparent noodles until soft. Cut the cabbage or greens into small pieces. Finely shred the ginger root and spring onions.

Heat the oil in a wok, frying pan or casserole, and fry the meat balls over a moderate heat until golden then remove with a perforated spoon. Add the ginger root and spring onions to the pan, followed by the cabbage and mushrooms, and fry.

Add the salt, stir a few times, then add the meat balls and the transparent noodles. Moisten with a little stock or water if necessary and bring to the boil. Reduce the heat, cover and simmer gently for about 20 to 25 minutes.

Serve with boiled rice.

Pork meat balls with vegetables

Lamb and spring onions

Metric	*Imperial*
225 g lamb fillet	8 oz lamb fillet
1×15 ml spoon soy sauce	1 tablespoon soy sauce
1×15 ml spoon sherry	1 tablespoon sherry
15 g dried wooden ears (optional)	½ oz dried wooden ears (optional)
100 g leeks	4 oz leeks
100 g spring onions	4 oz spring onions
2 slices ginger root, peeled	2 slices ginger root, peeled
4×15 ml spoons oil	4 tablespoons oil
2×5 ml spoons salt	2 teaspoons salt
1×5 ml spoon sugar	1 teaspoon sugar
3×15 ml spoons Stock (page 13) or water	3 tablespoons Stock (page 13) or water
1×5 ml spoon sesame seed oil	1 teaspoon sesame seed oil

Preparation time: 20 to 25 minutes

Cut the lamb into thin slices about the size of a large postage stamp, mix with the soy sauce and the sherry. Soak the wooden ears in warm water for 15 minutes, then rinse and discard any hard stalks. Cut the wooden ears into small pieces. Cut the leeks, spring onions and ginger root into 2.5 cm (1 inch) lengths.
Heat half the oil in a wok or frying pan and stir-fry the lamb for about 1 minute, then remove with a perforated spoon and put aside.
Heat the remaining oil in the pan, add the spring onions, leeks, ginger root, wooden ears, salt and sugar, followed by the lamb. Blend well together and add a little stock or water if necessary. Add the sesame seed oil and serve immediately.

Braised lamb chops

Metric	*Imperial*
450 g lamb chops	1 lb lamb chops
2 slices ginger root, peeled	2 slices ginger root, peeled
2 spring onions	2 spring onions
1×15 ml spoon oil	1 tablespoon oil
2×15 ml spoons sherry	2 tablespoons sherry
1×15 ml spoon brandy	1 tablespoon brandy
2×15 ml spoons soy sauce	2 tablespoons soy sauce
1×15 ml spoon sugar	1 tablespoon sugar
50 ml Stock (page 13) or water	2 fl oz Stock (page 13) or water

Preparation time: 5 to 10 minutes

Pork chops or T-bone steaks can also be cooked in this way and make a pleasant variation.

Trim off any excess fat from the chops. Finely shred the ginger root and cut the spring onions into 2.5 cm (1 inch) lengths.
Fry the chops in the oil for 10 to 15 seconds on each side. Transfer them to a saucepan or a flameproof casserole dish and add the sherry, brandy, soy sauce, sugar, ginger root and spring onions together with the stock or water. Cover and cook over a high heat for about 5 minutes (a little longer for pork but a little less for beef).
Serve with boiled rice and vegetables.

Stewed lamb

Metric	Imperial
750 g stewing lamb	1½-1¾ lb stewing lamb
1 garlic clove, crushed	1 garlic clove, crushed
2 slices ginger root, peeled	2 slices ginger root, peeled
2 spring onions	2 spring onions
2×15 ml spoons sherry	2 tablespoons sherry
1×2.5 ml spoon five-spice powder	½ teaspoon five-spice powder
3×15 ml spoons soy sauce	3 tablespoons soy sauce
1×15 ml spoon sugar	1 tablespoon sugar

From the left: Lamb and spring onions;
Braised lamb chops; Stewed lamb

Preparation time: 15 minutes

Cut the lamb into matchbox size pieces.
Place the cubes of lamb in a saucepan or flameproof casserole dish and add the crushed garlic, ginger root, spring onions and sherry, together with just enough water to cover. Bring it to the boil, then reduce the heat, cover and simmer for about 1 hour.
Add the five-spice powder, soy sauce and sugar and cook for a further 30 minutes or until there is almost no juice left. Serve hot.

Meat cubes in bean sauce: Cha shao

Cha shao (Cantonese barbecued pork)

Metric
1 kg pork fillet
1 × 15 ml spoon brandy
2 × 15 ml spoons sherry
2 × 15 ml spoons light soy
  sauce
1 × 15 ml spoon dark soy
  sauce
2 × 15 ml spoons Hoi Sin
  sauce
3 × 15 ml spoons clear
  honey

Imperial
2-2¼ lb pork fillet
1 tablespoon brandy
2 tablespoons sherry
2 tablespoons light soy
  sauce
1 tablespoon dark soy
  sauce
2 tablespoons Hoi Sin
  sauce
3 tablespoons clear
  honey

Preparation time: 10 to 15 minutes

Oven: 200°C, 400°F, Gas Mark 6

Traditionally, Cha Shao is served cold cut into thin slices crossways, or it can be used as an ingredient in a number of dishes such as Fried Rice (page 68) or Steamed Meat Dumplings (page 69).

Cut the pork into thin strips lengthwise. Mix together the brandy, sherry, soy sauce and Hoi Sin sauce and marinate the pork in this mixture for about 45 minutes.
To cook, lay the strips on a rack and roast in a moderately hot oven for 30 minutes, with a dish of water below to catch the fat. Remove from the oven and allow to cool for about 3 minutes before brushing each piece of meat with some of the clear honey. Return the meat to the oven and roast for a further 2 minutes or so.

Meat cubes in bean sauce

Metric
450 g pork fillet
1×15 ml spoon cornflour
oil for deep-frying

Imperial
1 lb pork fillet
1 tablespoon cornflour
oil for deep-frying

Sauce:
3×15 ml spoons crushed
  yellow bean sauce
3×15 ml spoons sugar

Sauce:
3 tablespoons crushed
  yellow bean sauce
3 tablespoons sugar

Preparation time: 10 minutes

Cut the meat into 1 cm (½ inch) cubes. Mix the cornflour with enough water to make a fairly thick paste and coat the meat cubes in it.
Heat the oil in a wok or frying pan and when hot, deep-fry the meat until lightly coloured (less than one minute). Remove with a perforated spoon and drain.
Pour off the excess oil, leaving about 1×15 ml spoon (1 tablespoon) in the wok or pan. Heat the oil until hot, then add the crushed yellow bean sauce combined with the sugar, stir a few times until it starts to bubble, then add the meat and blend well. When each cube is coated with sauce, arrange on a serving dish and serve.

Green peppers stuffed with pork

Metric
225 g pork, not too lean
4 water chestnuts
2 spring onions
1×2.5 ml spoon salt
1×15 ml spoon cornflour
225 g small green peppers
3×15 ml spoons oil
1×5 ml spoon sugar
2×15 ml spoons soy sauce
3×15 ml spoons Stock
  (page 13) or water

Imperial
8 oz pork, not too lean
4 water chestnuts
2 spring onions
½ teaspoon salt
1 tablespoon cornflour
8 oz small green peppers
3 tablespoons oil
1 teaspoon sugar
2 tablespoons soy sauce
3 tablespoons Stock
  (page 13) or water

Preparation time: 20 minutes

Finely chop the meat, the water chestnuts and spring onions and mix together with the salt and cornflour. Cut the peppers in half lengthways, or quarter them if large, remove the seeds.
Stuff the pepper halves with the pork mixture and sprinkle a little cornflour over.
Heat the oil in a frying pan. Lay the stuffed peppers in the pan, meat side down, and fry them for about 2 minutes, shaking the pan now and then gently to make sure the meat does not stick to the bottom of the pan. Add the sugar and soy sauce mixed with a little stock or water and simmer for 5 to 8 minutes. Carefully lift the peppers on to a dish, meat side up. Serve hot.

Green peppers stuffed with pork

51

Pork in bean sauce

Metric
450 g pork spare ribs
1 × 15 ml spoon soy sauce
2 × 15 ml spoons sherry
1 × 15 ml spoon sugar
1 × 15 ml spoon plain flour
2 spring onions
1 small green pepper, cored
  and seeded
1 small red pepper, cored
  and seeded
3 × 15 ml spoons oil
1 garlic clove, crushed
2 × 15 ml spoons crushed
  black or yellow bean
  sauce
5 × 15 ml spoons Stock
  (page 13) or water

Imperial
1 lb pork spare ribs
1 tablespoon soy sauce
2 tablespoons sherry
1 tablespoon sugar
1 tablespoon plain flour
2 spring onions
1 small green pepper, cored
  and seeded
1 small red pepper, cored
  and seeded
3 tablespoons oil
1 garlic clove, crushed
2 tablespoons crushed black
  or yellow bean
  sauce
5 tablespoons Stock
  (page 13) or water

Preparation time: 10 minutes

This is a very succulent dish. Ask your butcher to chop the meat into small pieces.

Mix the soy sauce, sherry, sugar and flour together and marinate the chopped spare ribs in this mixture for about 10 to 15 minutes.
Cut the spring onions into 2.5 cm (1 inch) lengths and finely slice the green and red peppers.
Heat the oil in a wok or frying pan and stir-fry the spare ribs until golden, then remove with a perforated spoon. Add the crushed garlic, the spring onions and the crushed black or yellow bean sauce to the wok or frying pan and stir. Add the spare ribs and blend well.
Add a little stock or water, place a lid on the wok or frying pan and cook over a high heat for 5 minutes. Add a little more stock or water if necessary, then replace the lid and cook for a further 5 minutes. Finally, add the green and red peppers, stir a few more times and serve hot.

Pork in bean sauce; Red-cooked pork; Pork and cucumber

Pork and cucumber

Metric	Imperial
225 g pork fillet	8 oz pork fillet
1 ×15 ml spoon sherry	1 tablespoon sherry
1 ×5 ml spoon cornflour	1 teaspoon cornflour
½ cucumber	½ cucumber
3 ×15 ml spoons oil	3 tablespoons oil
1 ×5 ml spoon salt	1 teaspoon salt
1 ×5 ml spoon sugar	1 teaspoon sugar
1 ×15 ml spoon soy sauce	1 tablespoon soy sauce
1 ×5 ml spoon sesame seed oil (optional)	1 tablespoon sesame seed oil (optional)

Preparation time: 15 to 20 minutes

Cut the pork into thin slices about the size of a large postage stamp. Mix the slices with the sherry and the cornflour.
Cut the cucumber into slices about the same size as the pork.
Heat the oil in a wok or frying pan and stir-fry the cucumber slices for 1 minute. Add the pork followed by the salt, sugar and soy sauce, continue stirring for 2 to 3 minutes. Finally, add the sesame seed oil, blend well and serve.

Red-cooked pork

Metric	Imperial
1 kg pork, cut into 4 cm cubes	2-2¼ lb pork, cut into 1½ inch cubes
1 garlic clove, crushed	1 garlic clove, crushed
4 ×15 ml spoons soy sauce	4 tablespoons soy sauce
3 ×15 ml spoons sherry	3 tablespoons sherry
50 g candy sugar or coffee sugar crystals	2 oz candy sugar or coffee sugar crystals
1 ×5 ml spoon five-spice powder	1 teaspoon five-spice powder

Preparation time: 20 minutes

Place the pork cubes in a saucepan or flameproof casserole dish with enough water to cover. Add the remaining ingredients, and bring to the boil over a high heat. Reduce the heat, cover and simmer gently for 1 to 1½ hours. There will only be a little liquid left at the end and this makes an excellent gravy.
Serve hot with rice and vegetables.

Sliced beef in oyster sauce

Metric
225 g beef steak
2 × 15 ml spoons oyster sauce
1 × 15 ml spoon sherry
1 × 15 ml spoon cornflour
100 g broccoli
100 g bamboo shoots
1 carrot, peeled
100 g fresh button
  mushrooms or 3-4
  Chinese dried mushrooms
2 slices ginger root, peeled
2 spring onions
4 × 15 ml spoons oil
1 × 5 ml spoon salt
1 × 5 ml spoon sugar
2 × 15 ml spoons Stock
  (page 13) or water

Imperial
8 oz beef steak
2 tablespoons oyster sauce
1 tablespoon sherry
1 tablespoon cornflour
4 oz broccoli
4 oz bamboo shoots
1 carrot, peeled
4 oz fresh button mushrooms
  or 3-4 Chinese dried
  mushrooms
2 slices ginger root, peeled
2 spring onions
4 tablespoons oil
1 teaspoon salt
1 teaspoon sugar
2 tablespoons Stock
  (page 13) or water

Preparation time: 20 to 25 minutes

Oyster sauce is a Cantonese speciality. The vegetables used in this recipe can be varied according to seasonal availability.

Cut the beef into thickish slices about the size of a matchbox. Mix together the oyster sauce, sherry and cornflour, and marinate the meat in this mixture for about 20 minutes.
Cut the broccoli into small florets, and the bamboo shoots and carrot into slices the same size as the beef as far as possible.
The button mushrooms can be left whole, but if you are using Chinese dried mushrooms, soak them in warm water for about 20 minutes, squeeze dry, discard the hard stalks and finely slice the mushrooms. Shred the ginger root and spring onions.
Heat about half the oil in a wok or frying pan and stir-fry the beef for about 10 to 15 seconds, then remove with a perforated spoon.
Heat the remaining oil in the wok or frying pan, then add the ginger root and the spring onions, followed by all the vegetables. Add the salt and sugar, stir and cook for about 1½ minutes. Add the beef, blend well together and add a little stock or water if necessary. Serve hot.

Lamb in sweet and sour sauce

Metric
275 g lamb fillet
1 × 5 ml spoon cornflour
1 × 15 ml spoon crushed
  yellow bean sauce
600 ml oil for deep-frying
2 slices ginger root, peeled
  and finely chopped
½ cucumber, sliced, to
  garnish

Imperial
10 oz lamb fillet
1 teaspoon cornflour
1 tablespoon crushed
  yellow bean sauce
1 pint oil for deep-frying
2 slices ginger root, peeled
  and finely chopped
½ cucumber, sliced, to
  garnish

Sauce:
1 × 15 ml spoon soy sauce
2 × 15 ml spoons sherry
1 × 15 ml spoon vinegar
2 × 15 ml spoons sugar
1 × 15 ml spoon cornflour
1 × 5 ml spoon sesame seed
  oil

Sauce:
1 tablespoon soy sauce
2 tablespoons sherry
1 tablespoon vinegar
2 tablespoons sugar
1 tablespoon cornflour
1 teaspoon sesame seed
  oil

Preparation time: 15 minutes

This is the original sweet and sour sauce recipe from northern China where lamb is more popular than pork.

Cut the lamb into thin slices about the size of an oblong postage stamp. Marinate the slices in the cornflour and the crushed yellow bean sauce for about 10 minutes.
Heat the oil in a wok or saucepan and deep-fry the lamb slices for about 20 seconds, stirring to separate each piece. When the slices are lightly coloured, remove them with a perforated spoon and drain.
Pour off the excess oil, leaving about ½ × 15 ml spoon (½ tablespoon) in the wok, toss in the ginger root, and the lamb slices. Add the soy sauce, sherry, vinegar, sugar and cornflour. Stir and blend for about 1 minute. Add the sesame seed oil and stir a few more times.
Serve hot, garnished with cucumber slices.

From the front, clockwise: Sliced beef in oyster sauce;
Lamb in sweet and sour sauce; Beef and onions

Beef and onions

Metric
225 g beef steak
1½×15 ml spoons soy sauce
1×15 ml spoon sherry
1×15 ml spoon cornflour
3×15 ml spoons oil
2 slices ginger root, peeled
225 g onions, peeled
1×5 ml spoon salt

Imperial
8 oz beef steak
1½ tablespoons soy sauce
1 tablespoon sherry
1 tablespoon cornflour
3 tablespoons oil
2 slices ginger root, peeled
8 oz onions, peeled
1 teaspoon salt

Preparation time: 20 to 30 minutes

Cut the beef into thin slices about the size of a large postage stamp. Mix the beef with the soy sauce, sherry and cornflour and leave the mixture to marinate for about 20 minutes.
Roughly chop the slices of ginger root and thinly slice the onion.
Heat the oil in a wok or frying pan until hot, then add the ginger root and sliced onion and stir. Add the salt and stir a few more times. Add the beef, stir constantly and keep the heat high. As soon as the thinly sliced beef pieces have separated from each other, arrange them on a hot serving dish and serve at once.

VEGETABLES

The Chinese eat more vegetables than they do meat or poultry and, apart from a few exceptions, most meat, fish and poultry dishes include some kind of vegetable. This is simple to understand when one considers the size of the country – approximately that of Western Europe or the United States of America – and range of climates available in China which encourage the growth of innumerable varieties of vegetables. You may find basic similarities between the Chinese and the Western methods of cooking fish and meat, but the Chinese style of cooking vegetables is quite unique. All the ingredients are stir-fried, that is to say tossed and mixed in a little hot oil over a high heat for a very short time, a practice which preserves the flavour and texture of the vegetables as well as their vitamins and the brightness of their colours.

The Chinese attach great importance to the freshness of ingredients when cooking vegetables and, ideally, they should be picked just before needed, but that is almost impossible unless you grow your own. However, always buy crisp, firm vegetables and cook them as soon as possible. Another point to remember is always wash the vegetables just before cutting them in order to avoid losing vitamins in water and, finally, cook them as soon as they have been cut so that the vitamin content is not lost through evaporation.

Tomatoes with onions and green peppers

Metric	Imperial
1 large or 2 small onions, peeled	1 large or 2 small onions, peeled
1 large or 2 small green peppers, cored and seeded	1 large or 2 small green peppers, cored and seeded
1 large or 2 small hard tomatoes	1 large or 2 small hard tomatoes
3 × 15 ml spoons oil	3 tablespoons oil
1 × 5 ml spoon salt	1 teaspoon salt
1 × 5 ml spoon sugar	1 teaspoon sugar

Preparation time: 10 minutes

Cut the onions, green peppers and tomatoes into uniform slices.

Heat the oil in a wok or frying pan and stir-fry the onions for 30 seconds, add the green peppers and continue cooking for about 1 minute. Add the tomatoes, salt and sugar. Cook for 1 minute more. Serve hot or cold.

Broccoli pieces in oyster sauce

Metric
225 g broccoli
3 ×15 ml spoons oil
2 ×15 ml spoons oyster
  sauce
2 ×15 ml spoons Stock
  (page 13) or water

Imperial
8 oz broccoli
3 tablespoons oil
2 tablespoons oyster
  sauce
2 tablespoons Stock
  (page 13) or water

Preparation time: 10 minutes

Cut the broccoli into small pieces. Remove the rough skin from the stalks, which, incidentally, are delicious to eat.
Heat the oil in a wok or frying pan until hot and stir-fry the broccoli for about 1 to 1½ minutes. Add the oyster sauce and a little stock or water and cook for a further 2 minutes. Serve hot.

Tomatoes with onions and green peppers;
Broccoli pieces in oyster sauce; Fried courgettes

Fried courgettes

Metric
450 g courgettes
3 ×15 ml spoons oil
2 ×5 ml spoons salt
1 ×5 ml spoon sugar
2 ×15 ml spoons Stock
  (page 13) or water

Imperial
1 lb courgettes
3 tablespoons oil
2 teaspoons salt
1 teaspoon sugar
2 tablespoons Stock
  (page 13) or water

Preparation time: 10 minutes

Marrow can be substituted for courgettes in this recipe, if peeled and cut into small cubes. It should be cooked for 2 minutes longer.
Do not peel the courgettes, just trim off the ends. Split the courgettes in half lengthwise, then cut each length diagonally into diamond-shaped chunks.
Heat the oil in a wok or frying pan and stir-fry the courgettes for about 30 seconds, then add the salt and sugar and cook for a further 1 to 1½ minutes, adding a little stock or water if necessary.
Courgettes are best eaten when slightly underdone, so do try not to overcook them. Serve hot.

Celery salad; Bean-sprout salad

Celery salad

Metric
1 celery stick
1 small green pepper, cored
  and seeded
1 ×5 ml spoon salt
2.25 litres water

Dressing:
2 ×15 ml spoons soy sauce
1 ×15 ml spoon vinegar
1 ×15 ml spoon sesame seed
  oil
1 slice ginger root, peeled
  and finely shredded, to
  garnish

Imperial
1 celery stick
1 small green pepper, cored
  and seeded
1 teaspoon salt
4 pints water

Dressing:
2 tablespoons soy sauce
1 tablespoon vinegar
1 tablespoon sesame seed
  oil
1 slice ginger root, peeled
  and finely shredded, to
  garnish

Preparation time: 15 to 20 minutes

Thinly slice the celery diagonally. Thinly slice the
green pepper. Place them both in a pan of boiling,
salted water for 1 to 2 minutes only. Pour them into
a colander and rinse in cold water until cool. Drain.
Mix together the ingredients for the dressing and
pour it over the celery and green pepper, toss well,
then garnish the salad with the finely shredded
ginger root and serve.

Bean-sprout salad

Metric
450 g fresh bean-sprouts
1 ×5 ml spoon salt
2.25 litres water

Dressing:
2 ×15 ml spoons soy sauce
1 ×15 ml spoon vinegar
1 ×15 ml spoon sesame seed
  oil
50 g cooked ham or
  chicken, finely sliced, to
  garnish

Imperial
1 lb fresh bean-sprouts
1 teaspoon salt
4 pints water

Dressing:
2 tablespoons soy sauce
1 tablespoon vinegar
1 tablespoon sesame seed
  oil
2 oz cooked ham or
  chicken, finely sliced, to
  garnish

Preparation time: 10 to 15 minutes

The Chinese seldom eat raw food, their 'salads'
consist of vegetables which are blanched, then
cooled in cold water and mixed in a dressing.

Wash and rinse the bean-sprouts in a basin of cold
water, discarding the husks and other bits and
pieces that float to the surface (it is not necessary to
top and tail each sprout).
Place the sprouts in a pan of boiling, salted water
and cook for 1 to 2 minutes only. Pour them into a
colander and rinse in cold water until cool. Drain.
Mix together the ingredients for the dressing and
pour it over the sprouts, stir and let it stand for 10
to 20 minutes. Garnish with cooked ham or chicken.

Fried lettuce

Metric
1 large cos lettuce
2–3 ×15 ml spoons oil
1 ×5 ml spoon salt
1 ×5 ml spoon sugar

Imperial
1 large cos lettuce
2–3 tablespoons oil
1 teaspoon salt
1 teaspoon sugar

Preparation time: 5 minutes

Discard the tough outer leaves and wash the lettuce well. Tear the larger leaves into 2 or 3 pieces, shaking off the excess water.
Heat the oil in a wok or large saucepan, add the salt followed by the lettuce leaves and stir vigorously as though tossing a salad. Add the sugar and continue stirring. As soon as the leaves become slightly limp quickly transfer them to a serving dish and serve.

Chinese cabbage and mushrooms

Metric
6–8 Chinese dried
   mushrooms
450 g Chinese cabbage
   leaves
3 ×15 ml spoons oil
1 ×5 ml spoon salt
1 ×5 ml spoon sugar
1 ×15 ml spoon soy sauce
1 ×5 ml spoon sesame seed
   oil

Imperial
6–8 Chinese dried
   mushrooms
1 lb Chinese cabbage
   leaves
3 tablespoons oil
1 teaspoon salt
1 teaspoon sugar
1 tablespoon soy sauce
1 teaspoon sesame seed
   oil

Preparation time: 15 minutes

Soak the mushrooms in warm water for about 20 minutes, then squeeze dry and discard the hard stalks. Cut each mushroom in half or into quarters depending on the size. Cut the cabbage leaves into pieces about the size of a large postage stamp.
Heat the oil in a wok or frying pan and stir-fry the cabbage and the mushrooms until soft. Add the salt, sugar and soy sauce and cook for a further 1½ minutes. Stir in a little of the water in which the mushrooms soaked, then add the sesame seed oil.

Spinach and Bean-curd Variation:
Stir-fry 2 cakes roughly chopped bean-curd in half the oil, then remove. Wash and stir-fry 225 g (8 oz) spinach in the remaining oil with the salt and sugar, for about 1 minute. Add the bean-curd and the soy sauce, blend well and cook for 1-2 minutes. Add the sesame seed oil and serve.

Fried lettuce; Chinese cabbage and mushrooms

Family-style bean-curd

Metric
4 cakes of bean-curd
100 g pork fillet
1 leek
5–6 dried red chillis
4×15 ml spoons oil
1×15 ml spoon sherry
1×15 ml spoon soy sauce
2×15 ml spoons crushed
  yellow bean sauce
1×5 ml spoon sesame seed
  oil

Imperial
4 cakes of bean-curd
4 oz pork fillet
1 leek
5–6 dried red chillis
4 tablespoons oil
1 tablespoon sherry
1 tablespoon soy sauce
2 tablespoons crushed
  yellow bean sauce
1 teaspoon sesame seed
  oil

Preparation time: 15 to 20 minutes

Bean-curd is rather bland on its own, but cooked in this way it is very tasty.

Cut each cake of bean-curd into 3 thin slices crossways, then cut each slice diagonally into 2 triangles. Cut the pork into thin shreds about the size of matchsticks. Cut the leek diagonally into chunks. Finely chop the dried red chillis.
Heat 3×15 ml spoons (3 tablespoons) of the oil in a wok or frying pan until hot, then fry the bean-curd pieces for about 2 minutes, turning once. Remove with a perforated spoon and drain.
Add the remaining oil, and stir-fry the red chillis, leek and pork. Add the sherry, soy sauce, bean-curd and crushed bean sauce, cook together for about 3 minutes, then add the sesame seed oil and serve.

Fried cauliflower

Metric	Imperial
1 cauliflower	1 cauliflower
3×15 ml spoons oil	3 tablespoons oil
2×5 ml spoons salt	2 teaspoons salt
1×5 ml spoon sugar	1 teaspoon sugar
4×15 ml spoons Stock (page 13) or water	4 tablespoons Stock (page 13) or water

Preparation time: 10 minutes

Wash the cauliflower in cold water, discarding the tough outer leaves and cut it into florets with part of the stalk still attached.
Heat the oil in a wok or frying pan and stir-fry the cauliflower for about 1 minute, then add the salt, sugar and stock or water. Cook for a further 2 minutes if you prefer your vegetables underdone, otherwise cook for 5 minutes, adding a little stock or water if necessary. Serve hot.

Family-style bean-curd; Fried cauliflower;
Mushrooms in oyster sauce

Mushrooms in oyster sauce

Metric	Imperial
450 g fresh button mushrooms	1 lb fresh button mushrooms
3×15 ml spoons oil	3 tablespoons oil
2×15 ml spoons oyster sauce	2 tablespoons oyster sauce
2×5 ml spoons cornflour	2 teaspoons cornflour
2×15 ml spoons Stock (page 13)	2 tablespoons Stock (page 13)
1×5 ml spoon sesame seed oil	1 teaspoon sesame seed oil
finely chopped fresh Chinese or English parsley, to garnish	finely chopped fresh Chinese or English parsley, to garnish

Preparation time: 10 to 15 minutes

Clean the mushrooms but do not peel them.
Heat the oil in a wok or frying pan and stir-fry the mushrooms for about 1½ minutes, add the oyster sauce and continue cooking for 1 minute.
Mix the cornflour to a paste with the stock and add this to the mushrooms. When the gravy thickens, add the sesame seed oil and blend well. Transfer to a serving dish, garnish with finely chopped Chinese parsley and serve.

Braised aubergines; Aubergines in fragrant sauce

Aubergines in fragrant sauce

Metric
225 g aubergines
100 g pork fillet
2 spring onions
1 slice ginger root, peeled
1 garlic clove, peeled
600 ml oil for deep-frying
1 × 15 ml spoon soy sauce
1 × 15 ml spoon sherry
2 × 5 ml spoons chilli purée
2 × 15 ml spoons cornflour

Imperial
8 oz aubergines
4 oz pork fillet
2 spring onions
1 slice ginger root, peeled
1 garlic clove, peeled
1 pint oil for deep-frying
1 tablespoon soy sauce
1 tablespoon sherry
2 teaspoons chilli purée
2 tablespoons cornflour

Preparation time: 20 minutes

Peel the aubergines, then cut them into strips about the size of potato chips.

Cut the pork into thin shreds the size of matchsticks.

Finely chop the spring onions, ginger root and garlic.

Heat the oil in a wok or saucepan and deep fry the aubergine 'chips' for about 1 or 2 minutes. Remove with a perforated spoon and drain.

Pour off the excess oil, leaving about 1 × 15 ml spoon (1 tablespoon) in the wok or pan and quickly stir-fry the spring onions, ginger root and garlic, followed by the pork. Add the soy sauce, sherry and chilli purée, blend well. Add the aubergine 'chips' and cook together for 1 to 2 minutes. Combine the cornflour with a little water and pour it into the wok or saucepan. Stir a few more times until the juice thickens, then serve hot.

Braised aubergines

Metric
275 g aubergines
600 ml oil for deep-frying
2×15 ml spoons soy sauce
1×15 ml spoon sugar
2×15 ml spoons Stock
  (page 13) or water
1×5 ml spoon sesame seed
  oil

Imperial
10 oz aubergines
1 pint oil for deep-frying
2 tablespoons soy sauce
1 tablespoon sugar
2 tablespoons Stock
  (page 13) or water
1 teaspoon sesame seed
  oil

Preparation time: 10 minutes

Choose the long, purple variety of aubergine, rather than the large round kind if possible.

Discard the stalks and cut the aubergines into diamond-shaped chunks.
Heat the oil in a wok or saucepan until hot and deep-fry the aubergine chunks in batches until golden, then remove with a perforated spoon and drain. Pour off the excess oil, leaving about 1×15 ml spoon (1 tablespoon) in the wok. Return the aubergines to the pan, add the soy sauce, sugar and the stock or water. Cook for about 2 minutes over a fairly high heat, adding more stock or water if necessary and stirring occasionally. When the juice is reduced to almost nothing, add the sesame seed oil, blend well and serve.

Braised bamboo shoots

Metric
4–5 Chinese dried
  mushrooms
275 g bamboo shoots
2 spring onions
3×15 ml spoons oil
1×15 ml spoon sherry
1×15 ml spoon soy sauce
2×5 ml spoons cornflour
50 g ham, finely chopped,
  to garnish

Imperial
4–5 Chinese dried
  mushrooms
10 oz bamboo shoots
2 spring onions
3 tablespoons oil
1 tablespoon sherry
1 tablespoon soy sauce
2 teaspoons cornflour
2 oz ham, finely chopped,
  to garnish

Preparation time: 10 minutes

Soak the mushrooms in warm water for 15 to 20 minutes, squeeze dry and discard the hard stalks, then cut each mushroom into 4 or 5 slices. Cut the bamboo shoots into strips the size of potato chips. Finely chop the spring onions.
Heat the oil in a wok or frying pan, add the spring onions, mushrooms and bamboo shoots and stir-fry for about 1 minute, then add the sherry and soy sauce. Continue to cook for a further minute, adding a little stock or water if necessary. Mix the cornflour with a little cold water and add to the wok or pan, stirring until the juice thickens. Serve immediately, garnished with the chopped ham.

Braised bamboo shoots

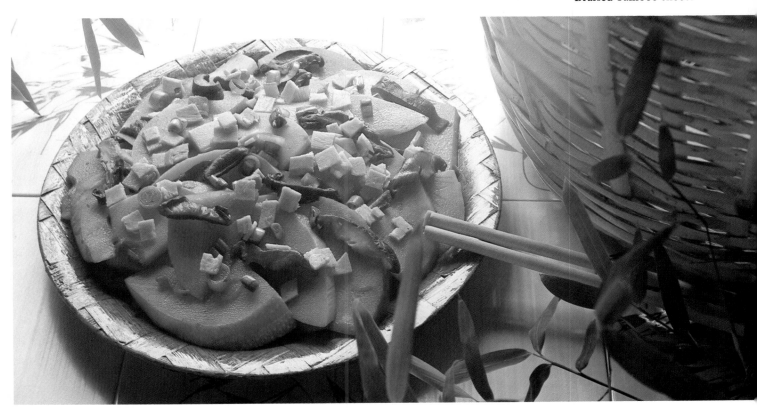

Mixed vegetables

Metric	Imperial
3–4 Chinese dried mushrooms	3–4 Chinese dried mushrooms
10 g wooden ears (optional)	¼ oz wooden ears (optional)
50 g bamboo shoots	2 oz bamboo shoots
50 g fresh bean-sprouts	2 oz fresh bean-sprouts
50 g fresh mushrooms	2 oz fresh mushrooms
50 g mange-tout peas or French beans	2 oz mange-tout peas or French beans
50 g broccoli or cauliflower	2 oz broccoli or cauliflower
50 g carrots	2 oz carrots
4×15 ml spoons oil	4 tablespoons oil
2×5 ml spoons salt	2 teaspoons salt
1×15 ml spoon sugar	1 tablespoon sugar
1×15 ml spoon soy sauce	1 tablespoon soy sauce
1×15 ml spoon cornflour	1 tablespoon cornflour
2×5 ml spoons sesame seed oil	2 teaspoons sesame seed oil

Preparation time: 25 to 30 minutes

The most important point in selecting the various ingredients for this dish is the balance of contrasting colours, textures and flavours. If, because of seasonal availability some fresh vegetable substitutes have to be made, make sure they are compatible with each other.

Soak the dried mushrooms and the wooden ears in separate bowls for about 25 minutes, then squeeze dry the mushrooms and discard the hard stalks. Rinse the wooden ears and discard any hard bits.
Cut the bamboo shoots into slices the size of a large postage stamp.
Wash the bean-sprouts in a basin of cold water, discarding the husks and other bits and pieces that float to the surface.
Wash the fresh mushrooms, leave them whole if small, otherwise cut each into 2 to 4 pieces.
Chop the rest of the fresh vegetables into roughly a uniform size.
Heat about half of the oil in a wok or frying pan and stir-fry the dried mushrooms, wooden ears, bamboo shoots and bean-sprouts for about 1 minute. Add the sugar, soy sauce and half the salt, stir for a little while, then remove with a perforated spoon and set the mixture aside.
Clean the wok or pan, heat the remaining oil and stir-fry the fresh vegetables. Add the salt and sugar and cook for about 1½ minutes, then mix in the partly cooked items. Cook together for a few seconds, then pour in the cornflour combined with a little water and the remaining soy sauce. Blend everything well together. Add the sesame seed oil and serve either hot or cold.

Chinese cabbage in a creamy sauce

Metric	Imperial
450 g Chinese cabbage	1 lb Chinese cabbage
4×15 ml spoons oil	4 tablespoons oil
1½×5 ml spoons salt	1½ teaspoons salt
1×5 ml spoon sugar	1 teaspoon sugar
50 ml Stock (page 13) or water	2 fl oz Stock (page 13) or water
1×15 ml spoon cornflour	1 tablespoon cornflour
4×15 ml spoons milk	4 tablespoons milk

Preparation time: 10 minutes

Cut each cabbage leaf into quarters.
Heat 3×15 ml spoons (3 tablespoons) oil in a wok or frying pan and stir-fry the cabbage for about 3 minutes. Add the salt and sugar, blend well until the cabbage softens, then remove with a perforated spoon and set aside.
Heat the remaining oil, add the stock and bring it to the boil. Meanwhile, mix the cornflour to a smooth paste with the milk and a little water, then add this to the stock and stir for about 1 minute to make a smooth, creamy sauce.
Add the cooked cabbage to the sauce and mix thoroughly, then arrange on a serving dish and serve immediately.

Mixed vegetables; Sweet and sour cabbage; Chinese cabbage in a creamy sauce

Sweet and sour cabbage

Metric
450 g white cabbage
1 green pepper, cored and seeded
1 red pepper, cored and seeded
3 × 15 ml spoons oil
6 dried hot chillis
12 peppercorns

Sauce:
2 × 15 ml spoons soy sauce
2 × 15 ml spoons vinegar
2 × 15 ml spoons sugar
1 × 5 ml spoon salt
1 × 15 ml spoon sesame seed oil, to garnish

Imperial
1 lb white cabbage
1 green pepper, cored and seeded
1 red pepper, cored and seeded
3 tablespoons oil
6 dried hot chillis
12 peppercorns

Sauce:
2 tablespoons soy sauce
2 tablespoons vinegar
2 tablespoons sugar
1 teaspoon salt
1 tablespoon sesame seed oil, to garnish

Preparation time: 10 minutes

Thinly shred the white cabbage and the green and red peppers.
Mix together the ingredients for the sauce.
Heat the oil in a wok or large frying pan and add the dried chillis and peppercorns. After a few seconds, add the cabbage and the green and red peppers, stir for about 1 to 1½ minutes, then pour in the sauce mixture and continue stirring until well blended.
Serve hot or cold, garnished with sesame seed oil.

EGG, RICE AND NOODLES

Poultry is plentiful in China and therefore eggs are very popular. However, they are used more as an ingredient in combination with other foods rather than served as a dish on their own, for instance: *Egg-Flower Soup (page 15); Prawns Fu-Yung (page 28)*.

It is a popular notion in the West that rice is the staple food of China, while this is certainly true in the southern part, people in Northern China eat far more wheat products such as dumplings for their everyday meals; and noodles either fried or in a soup are universally popular as snacks eaten between meals.

Braised eggs

Metric	Imperial
6 eggs	6 eggs

Sauce:	Sauce:
300 ml Stock (page 13)	½ pint Stock (page 13)
3×15 ml spoons soy sauce	3 tablespoons soy sauce
1×15 ml spoon sherry	1 tablespoon sherry
1×2.5 ml spoon five-spice powder	½ teaspoon five-spice powder
2 slices ginger root, peeled	2 slices ginger root, peeled

Preparation time: 5 minutes

Serve the braised eggs on their own, or as part of a mixed plate of cold meats such as *Soy Chicken* (page 37), *Cha Shao* (page 50).

The sauce left over from the *Soy Chicken* (page 37) or *Pork in Fragrant Sauce* (page 44), can be used in this dish, or make up a fresh one from a good stock.

To make the sauce, bring the stock gently to the boil in a saucepan and stir in the soy sauce, sherry, five-spice powder and ginger root.
Boil the eggs for about 5 minutes, then remove the shells. Simmer the eggs in the sauce over a gentle heat for 20 minutes, turning the eggs over now and again to ensure even cooking.
Leave the eggs to cool in the sauce. Just before serving, remove them with a perforated spoon and cut them into halves or quarters.

Spring rolls

Metric	Imperial
100 g pork fillet	4 oz pork fillet
1×15 ml spoon soy sauce	1 tablespoon soy sauce
1×15 ml spoon cornflour	1 tablespoon cornflour
100 g prawns, peeled	4 oz prawns, peeled
1 egg white	1 egg white
225 g fresh bean-sprouts	8 oz fresh bean-sprouts
4 spring onions	4 spring onions
3×15 ml spoons oil	3 tablespoons oil
1×5 ml spoon salt	1 teaspoon salt
6 eggs or 12 spring roll skins	6 eggs or 12 spring roll skins
1 litre oil for deep-frying	1¾ pints oil for deep-frying

Preparation time: 20 to 25 minutes

Finely shred the pork into slivers the size of a bean-sprout. Leave to marinate in soy sauce mixed with 1×5 ml spoon (1 teaspoon) of the cornflour.
Coarsely chop the peeled prawns. Leave them to marinate in the egg white mixed with 2×5 ml spoons (2 teaspoons) of the cornflour. Keep the prawn mixture in the refrigerator until needed.
Wash and rinse the bean-sprouts in a basin of cold water, discarding the husks and other bits and pieces that float to the surface.
Cut the spring onions into 2.5 cm (1 inch) lengths and slice them as thin as match-sticks.
Heat 2×15 ml (2 tablespoons) of the oil in a wok or frying pan and stir-fry the pork and prawns for 1 minute. Remove them with a perforated spoon and set aside. Heat the remaining oil in the pan until smoking, then stir-fry the bean sprouts and spring onions. Add the salt, followed by the pork and prawns. Stir constantly for about 1 to 2 minutes. Remove them with a perforated spoon and set aside.
If using eggs, beat them. Lightly grease the pan with oil. Place it over a low heat and pour in 2×15 ml spoons (2 tablespoons) of beaten egg. Tip the pan from side to side until a thin, round pancake forms. Transfer gently with a fish slice to a warm plate. Continue until you have made 12 pancakes.
Place about 3×15 ml spoons (3 tablespoons) pork and prawn filling on each spring roll pancake. Fold up the sides to make a tight roll and stick down the outer edges with a little flour and water paste.
Heat the oil in a wok or saucepan suitable for deep-frying and deep-fry the spring rolls a few at a time until golden. Crisp them in hot oil once more just before serving.

Braised eggs; Spring rolls

Plain rice

Metric
350 g long-grain rice
750 ml water

Imperial
12 oz long-grain rice
1¼ pints water

Preparation time: 5 minutes

Should you prefer your rice to be softer and less fluffy, then use the rounded, pudding rice and reduce the amount of water by a quarter.

Wash and rinse the rice in cold water.
Bring a pan of water to the boil over a high heat, add the washed rice and bring it back to the boil. Cover the pan tightly with a lid and reduce the heat. Cook gently for 20 minutes.
It is best not to serve the rice immediately but to leave it in the covered pan for 10 minutes. This ensures that the rice is not too sticky. Fluff it up with a fork or spoon before serving.

Fried rice

Metric
2 spring onions
3 eggs
1×5 ml spoon salt
4×15 ml spoons oil
50 g cooked ham or Cha Shao (page 50)
50 g cooked prawns, peeled
100 g green peas
4 cups cooked rice, or 175 g raw rice cooked in 500 ml water
1½×15 ml spoons soy sauce

Imperial
2 spring onions
3 eggs
1 teaspoon salt
4 tablespoons oil
2 oz cooked ham or Cha Shao (page 50)
2 oz cooked prawns, peeled
4 oz green peas
4 cups cooked rice, or 6 oz raw rice cooked in 18 fl oz water
1½ tablespoons soy sauce

Preparation time: 15 to 20 minutes

Finely chop the spring onions. Mix half of them with the eggs, add a pinch of salt and beat lightly.
Heat a third of the oil in a wok or frying pan, then add the eggs and stir until scrambled. When the eggs set, transfer them to a pre-heated plate and break them into small pieces with a fork.
Heat another third of the oil in the pan. Meanwhile dice the ham or pork to about the size of peas. Place the meat cubes, the prawns, peas and the remaining salt in the pan and stir-fry for about 1 minute then remove with a perforated spoon and set aside.
Heat the remaining oil in the pan, then add the spring onions and cooked rice. Stir to separate each grain of rice. Add the soy sauce and stir until it is evenly blended with the rice, then add the eggs, ham or pork, prawns and peas. Reduce the heat. Serve as soon as everything is well mixed.

Steamed meat dumplings

Metric
500 g plain flour
4×5 ml spoons baking
  powder
250 ml water

Imperial
1¼ lb plain flour
4 teaspoons baking
  powder
8 fl oz water

Filling:
450 g pork, not too lean
1×15 ml spoon sherry
3×15 ml spoons soy sauce
2×5 ml spoons sugar
1×5 ml spoon salt
1×15 ml spoon sesame seed
  oil
2×5 ml spoons peeled and
  finely chopped ginger
  root
1×5 ml spoon cornflour

Filling:
1 lb pork, not too lean
1 tablespoon sherry
3 tablespoons soy sauce
2 teaspoons sugar
1 teaspoon salt
1 tablespoon sesame seed
  oil
2 teaspoons peeled and
  finely chopped ginger
  root
1 teaspoon cornflour

Left: Plain rice; Fried rice
Above: Steamed meat dumplings

Preparation time: 1½ to 2 hours

Any left-over dumplings can be reheated either by steaming for 5 minutes or shallow-frying in a little oil for 6 to 7 minutes, turning over once during cooking.

Sift the flour and baking powder together in a mixing bowl. Add the water and knead well. Cover the bowl with a damp cloth and place a small plate over this, then leave the dough to rise at room temperature for 2 hours.
Mince the pork. Mix it with the sherry, soy sauce, sugar, salt, sesame seed oil, ginger root and cornflour.
Divide the dough in half, place on a lightly floured surface and knead. Make each half into a long sausage-like roll 5 cm (2 inches) in diameter. Use a knife to slice each roll into about 15 rounds. Flatten each round with the palm of your hand, then with a rolling pin, roll out each piece into a pancake about 7.5 cm (3 inches) in diameter.
Place 1×15 ml spoon (1 tablespoon) filling in the centre of each pancake, gather the sides of the dough up around the filling to meet at the top, then twist the top of the dough to close tightly.
Place a piece of wet muslin on a rack in a steamer, arrange the dumplings 1 cm (½ inch) apart on the muslin, cover and steam vigorously for 20 minutes. Serve hot.

From the front, clockwise: Soft noodles with crab meat sauce; Boiled noodles; Chow mein

Soft noodles with crab meat sauce

Metric
150 g egg noodles
pinch of salt
2×15 ml spoons oil
1 small can crab meat
 (about 100 g drained
 weight)
100 g greens (spinach or
 cabbage), cut into
 rough pieces
1×5 ml spoon soy sauce
250 ml Stock (page 13)
1 spring onion, finely
 chopped, to garnish

Imperial
5 oz egg noodles
pinch of salt
2 tablespoons oil
1 small can crab meat
 (about 4 oz drained
 weight)
4 oz greens (spinach or
 cabbage), cut into
 rough pieces
1 teaspoon soy sauce
8 fl oz Stock (page 13)
1 spring onion, finely
 chopped, to garnish

Preparation time: 15 to 20 minutes

Add the noodles to a saucepan of salted boiling water and boil for 5 minutes. Drain through a colander and keep warm in a serving dish.
Heat the oil in a wok or pan and stir-fry the crab meat and greens. Add the soy sauce and stock. Cook for 2 to 3 minutes, pour the mixture over the noodles, then garnish with finely chopped spring onion. Serve at once.
Serves at least 2.

Boiled noodles

Metric
300 g egg noodles
200 g chicken breast meat, boned
2×5 ml spoons cornflour
8 Chinese dried mushrooms or 225 g fresh mushrooms
225 g bamboo shoots
225 g spinach leaves
4 spring onions
2 slices ginger root, peeled
1 litre Stock (page 13)
8×15 ml spoons oil

Sauce:
8×15 ml spoons soy sauce
4×15 ml spoons sherry
2×5 ml spoons salt
2×5 ml spoons sugar

Imperial
11 oz egg noodles
7 oz chicken breast meat, boned
2 teaspoons cornflour
8 Chinese dried mushrooms or 8 oz fresh mushrooms
8 oz bamboo shoots
8 oz spinach leaves
4 spring onions
2 slices ginger root, peeled
1¾ pints Stock (page 13)
8 tablespoons oil

Sauce:
8 tablespoons soy sauce
4 tablespoons sherry
2 teaspoons salt
2 teaspoons sugar

Preparation time: 20 minutes

Bring a saucepan of water to the boil, add the noodles and simmer for 5 minutes until soft but not sticky. Drain them through a sieve and place in a large pre-heated bowl. Keep this warm.
Cut the chicken into matchstick-sized shreds. Mix the shreds with cornflour.
Soak the Chinese dried mushrooms in warm water for about 20 minutes, then squeeze dry and discard the hard stalks. Cut the Chinese mushrooms into thin shreds.
Wash the spinach well. Cut the bamboo shoots and the spinach into thin strips.
Finely chop the spring onions and the ginger root.
Bring the stock to the boil and then pour it over the cooked noodles.
Heat the oil in a wok or frying pan and add first the chicken, followed by the bamboo shoots, mushrooms, spinach, spring onions, and ginger root, in that order. Stir-fry the ingredients for about 1 minute. Mix together the sauce ingredients and pour into the pan. Continue stirring for another 1 to 2 minutes. Pour the mixture over the noodles and the stock and serve.

Chow mein

Metric
250 g egg noodles
275 g pork fillet
2×5 ml spoons cornflour
100 g bamboo shoots
100 g spinach leaves
½ cucumber
5×15 ml spoons oil

Sauce:
2×15 ml spoons soy sauce
1×15 ml spoon sherry
1×5 ml spoon salt
1×5 ml spoon sugar
1×5 ml spoon cornflour
1×5 ml spoon sesame seed oil, to garnish

Imperial
8 oz egg noodles
10 oz pork fillet
2 teaspoons cornflour
4 oz bamboo shoots
4 oz spinach leaves
½ cucumber
5 tablespoons oil

Sauce:
2 tablespoons soy sauce
1 tablespoon sherry
1 teaspoon salt
1 teaspoon sugar
1 teaspoon cornflour
1 teaspoon sesame seed oil, to garnish

Preparation time: 20 to 25 minutes

Bring a saucepan of water to the boil, add the noodles and simmer for five minutes until soft but not sticky. Drain in a sieve and rinse with cold water.
Cut the pork into shreds the size of a match-stick and mix them with the cornflour.
Cut the bamboo shoots, spinach and cucumber into thin shreds the same size as the pork.
Heat about half the oil in a wok or frying pan. Place the noodles in a large bowl, separating them with a fork, then pour over the hot oil.
Stir to ensure the noodles are evenly coated. Return them to the wok or pan and stir-fry for 2 to 3 minutes. Remove them with a perforated spoon and place on a serving dish.
Heat the remaining oil in the pan and stir-fry the bamboo shoots, cucumber, spinach, pork and cornflour. Mix together the sauce ingredients and pour into the pan. Cook for about 2 minutes, then pour the mixture over the noodles, garnish with sesame seed oil and serve.

Won ton soup

Metric
175 g minced pork
100 g spinach leaves,
    chopped
1×2.5 ml spoon salt
1×5 ml spoon sugar
1×15 ml spoon sherry
600 ml Stock (page 13)
24 Won ton skins (see
    right)
1 spring onion, finely
    chopped, to garnish

Imperial
6 oz minced pork
4 oz spinach leaves,
    chopped
½ teaspoon salt
1 teaspoon sugar
1 tablespoon sherry
1 pint Stock (page 13)
24 Won ton skins (see
    right)
1 spring onion, finely
    chopped, to garnish

Preparation time: 15 to 20 minutes

Serve this substantial soup as a main dish.

Mix the minced pork and chopped spinach leaves with the salt, sugar and sherry.
Place 1×5 ml spoon (1 teaspoon) of the meat and spinach mixture in the centre of each Won ton skin. Bring the opposite corners together in a fold. Seal by pinching the top edges together firmly. Fold the other two corners towards each other and seal.
Bring the stock to the boil, drop in the Won tons and boil rapidly for 2 to 3 minutes. Serve in individual bowls, garnished with chopped spring onions.

Won ton skins

Metric
1 egg
6×15 ml spoons water
225 g plain flour

Imperial
1 egg
6 tablespoons water
8 oz plain flour

Preparation time: 30 minutes

Should you be unable to obtain ready-made Won ton skins from your local stores, here is the recipe for making your own.

Lightly beat the egg and mix with the water in a bowl. Stir in the flour and knead together well until a smooth, stiff dough. Cover with a damp cloth and set aside for about 30 minutes.
Roll the dough out into a sheet about 1.5 mm (1/16 inch) thick, cut out about 24×2.5 cm (3 inch) squares. Dust each square lightly with flour.
If the Won ton skins are not to be used immediately, cover them with a damp cloth.

Egg fu-yung

Metric	*Imperial*
2 Chinese dried mushrooms or 50 g fresh mushrooms	*2 Chinese dried mushrooms or 2 oz fresh mushrooms*
25 g prawns, peeled	*1 oz prawns, peeled*
25 g cooked ham	*1 oz cooked ham*
25 g bamboo shoots	*1 oz bamboo shoots*
2–3 water chestnuts	*2–3 water chestnuts*
4 eggs, beaten	*4 eggs, beaten*
1×15 ml spoon cornflour	*1 tablespoon cornflour*
50 ml water	*2 fl oz water*
1×5 ml spoon salt	*1 teaspoon salt*
1×15 ml spoon sherry	*1 tablespoon sherry*
3×15 ml spoons oil	*3 tablespoons oil*

Preparation time: 15 minutes

This dish can also be served as a filling for pancakes.

Soak the dried mushrooms in warm water for about 20 minutes, then squeeze dry and discard the hard stalks. Finely chop the mushrooms, prawns, ham, bamboo shoots and water chestnuts. Mix together with the beaten eggs. Add the cornflour, water, salt and sherry to the egg mixture and stir.
Heat the oil in wok or frying pan until smoking, then pour in the egg mixture and scramble with a fork until the mixture sets. Serve hot.

Won ton soup; Won ton skins; Egg fu-yung

DESSERTS

The Chinese do not serve desserts or sweet dishes for everyday meals. The very limited range of Chinese desserts make their appearance only at formal banquets, and they are served not at the end but in between savoury dishes!
For those who are accustomed to finish off a meal with a dessert, fresh fruit or fruit salad is suggested, or canned or fresh lychees are always popular and would add an exotic touch to the occasion.

Steamed cake

Metric
2 eggs
50 g brown sugar
75 ml milk
100 g self-raising flour
1×15 ml spoon lard or
  vegetable fat
golden syrup, to serve

Imperial
2 eggs
2 oz brown sugar
3 fl oz milk
4 oz self-raising flour
1 tablespoon lard or
  vegetable fat
golden syrup, to serve

Eight-treasure rice pudding

Metric
225 g short grain rice
3×15 ml spoons lard
3×15 ml spoons sugar
15 dried red dates
30 raisins
10 walnuts
10 glacé cherries
1×15 ml spoon candied
  angelica, chopped

Filling:
1×225 g can sweetened
  chestnut purée

Syrup:
3×15 ml spoons sugar
300 ml water
1×15 ml spoon cornflour

Imperial
8 oz short grain rice
3 tablespoons lard
3 tablespoons sugar
15 dried red dates
30 raisins
10 walnuts
10 glacé cherries
1 tablespoon candied
  angelica, chopped

Filling:
1×8 oz can sweetened
  chestnut purée

Syrup
3 tablespoons sugar
½ pint water
1 tablespoon cornflour

Preparation time: 25 to 30 minutes

Beat the eggs in a mixing bowl, and stir in the sugar and milk. Fold in the sifted flour and mix together well.
Melt the lard, and when cool, add to the mixture.
Pour the mixture into a greased 20 cm (8 inch) cake tin and steam vigorously for 20 to 30 minutes.
Remove the cake from the tin while still hot. Cut into squares or triangles and serve either hot or cold with golden syrup.

Preparation time: 15 to 20 minutes

This is a festival dish traditionally served at New Year or other special occasions. The eight-treasures are eight different dried fruits and nuts representing eight objects of charm, which are supposed to ward off evil spirits. The recipe has been modified somewhat as some of the ingredients are unobtainable in the West.

Wash the rice in cold water. Place it in a saucepan and add enough water to cover. Bring to the boil, then reduce the heat, cover and simmer very gently for 10 to 15 minutes.
Mix 2×15 ml spoons (2 tablespoons) of the lard with the cooked rice and stir in the sugar.
Grease the bottom and side of a 900 ml (1½ pint) mould or pudding basin with the remaining lard. Cover the bottom and sides of the mould with a thin layer of cooked rice. Place a row of dates around the inside edge of the mould. Cover this with a layer of rice, then place a row of raisins on top. Cover with rice and layer with the remaining fruit and nuts, sandwiched between layers of rice. You will now have attractive rows of fruit and nuts around the edges with a hollow in the centre. Press gently to the sides of the mould so that the colours will show through when turned out for serving later on.
Cover the fruits and nuts with another layer of cooked rice, much thicker this time, then fill the centre with the chestnut purée and finally cover it with the rest of the rice. Press down gently to flatten the top.
Cover with tin foil and steam the pudding in a double boiler for about an hour.
Meanwhile, make the syrup. Dissolve the sugar in the water over gentle heat. When dissolved, increase the heat and boil for about 5 minutes. Thicken the syrup by stirring in the cornflour mixed with a little cold water.
Turn the pudding out on to a round dish, pour the syrup over it and serve hot.

Eight-treasure rice pudding; Steamed cake

Almond junket

Metric	Imperial
25 g gelatine powder	1 oz gelatine powder
4×15 ml spoons granulated sugar	4 tablespoons granulated sugar
150 ml evaporated milk	¼ pint evaporated milk
600 ml water	1 pint water
1×5 ml spoon almond essence	1 teaspoon almond essence
1×300 g can mandarins or cherries	1×11 oz can mandarins or cherries

Preparation time: 15 to 20 minutes
(excluding chilling time)

When served very cold this dessert is most refreshing to eat.

Dissolve the gelatine and the sugar in a saucepan of milk and water placed over a very gentle heat. Add the almond essence and pour the mixture into a large serving bowl. Let it cool for at least 30 minutes before placing it in the refrigerator for 3 hours to set.
To serve, cut the junket into small cubes, pour over the canned fruit and the syrup.

Toffee bananas

Metric	Imperial
4 bananas, peeled	4 bananas, peeled
1 egg	1 egg
2×15 ml spoons plain flour	2 tablespoons plain flour
600 ml oil for deep-frying	1 pint oil for deep-frying
4×15 ml spoons sugar	4 tablespoons sugar
1×15 ml spoon water	1 tablespoon water

Preparation time: 10 minutes

The batter mixture may be prepared well in advance of cooking. It is essential that the toffee-covered fruit is dipped into the water while very hot, so this can be done in the kitchen before serving.

Cut the bananas in half lengthwise, then cut each half into two.
Beat the egg, add the flour and mix to make a batter. Heat the oil in a wok or saucepan, coat each piece of banana with batter and deep fry until golden. Remove the banana with a perforated spoon and drain thoroughly.
Pour off the excess oil and leave about 1×15 ml spoon (1 tablespoon) oil in the wok or saucepan. Add the sugar and water and stir over a gentle heat to dissolve the sugar.
Increase the heat, and when the mixture becomes golden brown, quickly mix in the banana pieces, blend well and serve immediately.
Place a bowl of cold water on the table and dip each piece of banana into this to harden the toffee.

Almond junket

76

Toffee bananas; Toffee apples

Toffee apples

Metric	Imperial
4 large, firm eating apples, peeled and cored	4 large, firm eating apples, peeled and cored
4×15 ml spoons plain flour	4 tablespoons plain flour
1×15 ml spoon cornflour	1 tablespoon cornflour
2 egg whites	2 egg whites
1 litre oil for deep-frying	1¾ pints oil for deep-frying
100 g sugar	4 oz sugar
2×15 ml spoons water	2 tablespoons water
1×15 ml spoon lard	1 tablespoon lard
1×15 ml spoon sesame seeds	1 tablespoon sesame seeds

Preparation time: 15 minutes

Cut each apple into eight pieces. Sprinkle the pieces with a little of the flour. Mix the remaining flour with the cornflour and egg whites to make a batter. Heat the oil in a wok or saucepan, coat each piece of apple with batter, and deep-fry for about 3 minutes. Remove the apple pieces with a perforated spoon and drain them thoroughly.

Place the sugar and water in a saucepan and stir over a gentle heat. Add the lard, increase the heat and continue stirring until the sugar has caramelized. Add the apple pieces, stir, and add the sesame seeds. Serve as soon as they are well blended.

Place a bowl of cold water on the table and dip each piece of apple into this to harden the toffee before eating.

GARNISHES

Traditionally, the Chinese used garnishes on food mainly for formal banquets and in certain restaurants situated in seaports, notably Canton, where foreign influences were strong.
The attractive sculptured fruit and vegetable garnishes shown here can be easily made and used to enhance the colour, texture and flavour of the recipes in this book.

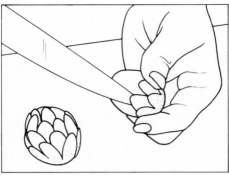

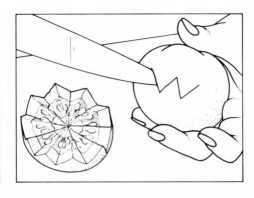

Radishes
For radish roses, cut off the root end and trim the top. Cut thin petals, starting at the stem end and finished at the root. Plunge them into iced water and leave for 1 hour. Drain, pat dry and use.

Tomatoes
For tomato lilies, insert a sharp knife into the tomato at an angle. Work round making 'v' cuts, then carefully separate the 2 halves, each half making an attractive flower shape.

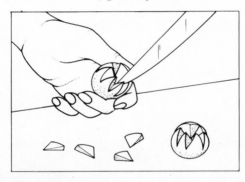

To make radish flowers, 'vandyke' a trimmed bulb by making 'v' cuts around the outside of the bulb towards the centre. Remove and discard the top.

For tomato roses, using a sharp knife peel off the skin, like an apple, in one piece. Curl the skin into a circle, then invert it.

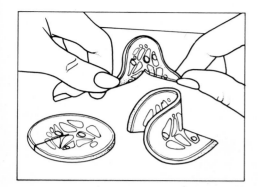

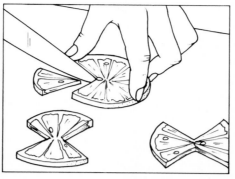

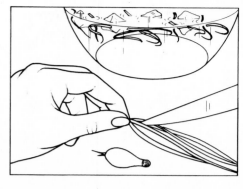

Cucumbers

For cucumber twists, thinly slice a cucumber leaving on the skin. Make one cut towards the centre. Twist both edges in opposite directions. Lemon twists are made in the same way.

Lemons

For lemon butterflies, cut a slice of lemon in half, then cut towards the centre leaving the centre intact. Remove and discard the cut flesh. The butterfly shapes can be used for either sweet or savoury dishes.

Spring onions

Trim off the bulb and white stem. Shred the green part into 5 cm/2 inch lengths. Leave plain, or make curls by plunging the strips into iced water. Drain, pat dry and use them immediately.

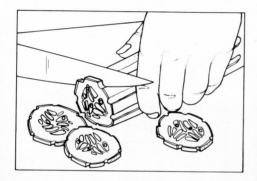

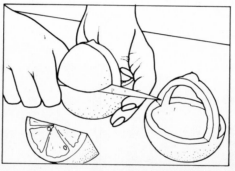

For cucumber cartwheels, use a sharp knife to cut small strips vertically from the peel at about 1 cm/½ inch intervals. Remove the cut peel. Cut the cucumber across into slices.

For lemon baskets, make a handle by cutting either side of the pointed end to two-thirds of the way down. Make a horizontal cut either side to meet the handle base. Remove all flesh.

To make spring onion fans, cut off the bulb end so that the stalk measures 7.5 cm/3 inches. Using a sharp knife, shred the green part to within 2.5 cm/1 inch of the white stem. Plunge the onions into iced water and leave for about 1 hour. Drain, pat dry and use immediately. These can be left in water for several hours.

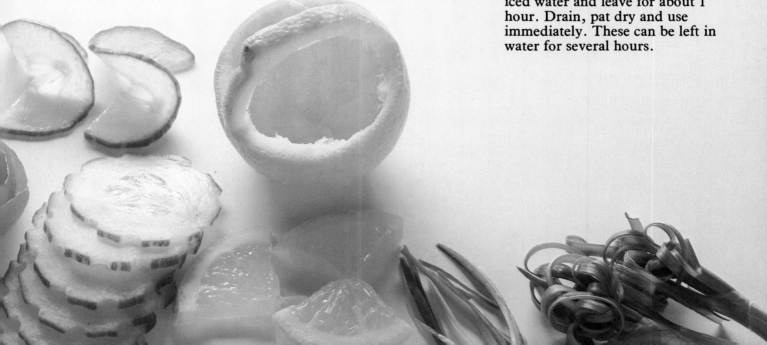

Index

ACKNOWLEDGEMENTS

The publishers would like to thank the following companies for their kindness in providing materials and equipment used in the photography for this book.

Neal Street Shop, Neal Street, Covent Garden, London WC2: ½ title page, pages 55 and 58 antique Cantonese dishes. The Conran Shop, 77-79 Fulham Road, London SW3: pages 12, 13 cream bowls; 14, 15 white peony bowls and bamboo tray (also page 17); 26, 27 white stem glasses. Elizabeth David, 46 Bourne Street, London SW1: pages 14, 15 white acid spoon; pages 60, 61 brown gratin earthenware dishes. David Mellor, 4 Sloane Square, London SW1: page 25 black plates.

The Chinese cooking utensils and crockery shown in this book are available from most Chinese supermarkets.

We should also like to thank the following who were concerned in the preparation of the book.

Photographer Bryce Attwell with stylist Roisin Nield

Chinese calligraphy by Chan Chien-ying